The Magic
of Ribbons

The Magic of Ribbons

Kay Anderson

Nexus Special Interests Ltd.
Nexus House
Azalea Drive
Swanley
Kent BR8 8HU
England

First published by Nexus Special Interests Ltd., 1998

ISBN 1-85486-186-7

Colour reproduction by PDQ Repro Ltd, Bungay, Suffolk
Designed and typeset by Kate Williams, Abergavenny
Printed and bound in Great Britain by Jarrold Book Printing, Thetford

For Alec
with all my love
You will always be my knight in shining armour

Contents

Acknowledgements

I would like to thank most sincerely:
Selectus Ltd. (for supplying all the beautiful
PANDA ribbons and the woven jacquards used
in this book)
Newey Goodman (for their haberdashery)
The Vilene Retail Organisation (for supplying all
the iron-on interfacing)
Wm. E. Wright Ltd. USA (for all the tassels and
braids)
Janome UK Ltd.

For help in preparing the history of the ribbon
weaving industry:
The Fashion Research Centre Museum of
Costume, Bath
Hugh Jones of the The Herbert Art Gallery,
Coventry
Sheila Shreeve for the historical fashion plates

Studio photography:
Jack Evans
Lindsay Chalford-Brown (illustrations on pages
70, 86, 96 and 97)
Jim Davies (illustrations on pages 45, 53 and 80)

Lindsay Chalford-Brown for her beautiful
illustrations of my fashion designs and for her
humour and encouragement.

For practical help with sewing projects:
Lynn Wright
Margaret Lawrence
Angela Thomas
Ann Olphin for her ribbon rose cards
Erva Legere for the boy's christening suit
Mary Day for the silk painted fabric for the
cushion and waistcoat
Wendy Crease for help in numerous ways

A very special thank you to all my family for their
love and support, to my parents who encouraged
me from childhood in every aspect of needlework
and design, my daughters in-law Amanda and
Louise, who allowed me to design and make their
wedding dresses. My Three Musketeers — my sons
Stephen, Andrew and Paul for their constant help,
love and support at all times and for modelling the
waistcoats in this book.

Introduction

The Magic of Ribbons will introduce you to a new concept with ribbon embellishment, shedding its purely craft image to one of elegant sophistication. Combined with braids, fabrics and tassels, ribbons can create rich opulent textures for your home furnishing, fashion and crafts.

My love of colour and texture is something I have been aware of since early childhood, stimulated, I think, by a kaleidoscope designed and made for me by my father. I still remember marvelling at the wonderful patterns produced by simply shaking the glass. In this book I aim to inspire you and to share with you the secrets of ribbon embellishment. By tastefully adding small areas of ribbon you will be able to create beautiful trimmings, adding colour and texture to your home and your fashions with style and panache that is simple to do – no experience is necessary.

Ribbons provide an easy and instant method of co-ordinating colour schemes – especially when decorating on a tight budget – and by learning the various techniques in the following pages you will become very creative. I will show you how to start with simple projects graduating to more intricate designs that can be passed on as family heirlooms. Ribbon work is very therapeutic as it grows fast and looks stunning.

I have included a historical background to give an insight into the ribbon weaving industry from the mid fourteenth century through to the twentieth century. I hope this will motivate readers of all ages to further reading and research into the work and skills of our ancestors, and to appreciate the richness of their beautiful work.

Since writing my first book *Fashion with Ribbon*, my journey with ribbon textiles has led me to travel far and wide, being privileged to demonstrate at public shows, trade shows and private groups, to students of all ages and as far afield as New Zealand and Australia, meeting many interesting people with fascinating hobbies. Motivating and inspiring my students has given me a wonderful opportunity to see the varied textures and colours they each produced. This in turn has encouraged me to develop the techniques further and to write this book. As you work through the pages you will find all the technical skills you need to enable you to produce the various weaves very quickly.

The desire to wear something new and different is born in us all. I have provided you with the framework on which your own ideas can be added to give full reign to your imagination. Let this book be a catalyst: use any of the techniques, expand on them and become your own designer.

I wish you much enjoyment from your new-found skills.

A Short History of the Ribbon Weaving Industry

The beautiful but practical ribbons we can buy today have evolved from an industry with a fascinatingly long and important history. Ribbon weaving was first reported in France in the mid-fourteenth century when women wove dress trimmings and sashes. Ribbon production gradually developed in certain areas; Paris, Lyons and St. Etienne (France), Krefeld (Germany), Basle (Switzerland), Vienna (Austria) and Coventry (England). However, it was not until the sixteenth century that ribbons in their present form were seen and heard of, and only in the seventeenth century that they acquired the fascination which has lasted through to the imaginative uses of today's fashionable, easy-care ribbons.

St. Etienne was a thriving ribbon-producing area in the early seventeenth century, helped by Henry 1V's recommendation to plant mulberry trees on French soil to cultivate the native silkworms. During the eighteenth century, French ribbon design dominated the European market: France was already exporting ribbons to England, mainly from St. Etienne, where the weavers produced brilliant designs of richly ornamented ribbons entwined with silver and gold lamé in the silk threads. Producing these ribbons was very costly, as the machinery was extremely complex, and it took several weeks to set up a loom before weaving could begin, however the early ribbon manufacturers were painstaking in their work and meticulous with their products, which were as rich as any hand embroidery. A great deal of this ribbon was produced for the court in Paris, also the Swedish and Russian courts. Other centres of the trade worked for a restricted market only. In the nineteenth century, ribbon industries grew in Paterson (USA), Moscow, Belgium and Spain. The competition became intense, the largest exporters being St. Etienne and Basle. The beautiful jacquard ribbons made in St. Etienne were exported to England, Germany, Belgium, Brazil, Chile, Mexico and Spain. St. Etienne, however, imported plain ribbons from Basle, which were the speciality of that city. At the London exhibition in 1851, several prizes were awarded to the Basle weavers.

Silk ribbon weaving began in Coventry in the late seventeenth century, with the influx of the Huguenots, the Protestant refugees fleeing from the French silk weaving area. At first, only plain ribbons were made, but such were the skills of these weavers that Coventry began to dominate the fancy end of the ribbon market, and in the eighteenth century the city and the area to the north became the most important centre for their manufacture in Britain.

During early Victorian times, Coventry was unique in its dependence on the ribbon industry, as at least a quarter of its population was employed as ribbon weavers. It was, in fact, the nineteenth century that enjoyed the greatest prosperity for the ribbon weavers, when the industry achieved worldwide importance.

Until the advent of steam, the mainstay of the ribbon industry was the outworker. The weavers collected the silk from the manufacturers and wove the ribbons in a room in their houses. However, following the introduction of steam, factories were established in Coventry. As an alternative to factories, some manufacturers built rows of topshop houses with steam power to run the looms, thus creating cottage factories. This was considered unique in Europe. For many years there was remarkable harmony between manufacturers and workers in Coventry, but during the 1860s this relationship deteriorated. This was due in part to disputes over list prices paid to the weavers and also to the reluctance of many workers to work in factories. The outcome was lockouts and strikes.

From the mid-1830s to 1860 the Coventry ribbon manufacturers enjoyed prosperity and progress, owing mainly to the introduction of a loom designed by Joseph Marie-Jacquard (1752–1834) of Lyons. Although in use on the continent since 1801, his automatic pattern selector did not arrive in England until 1823. However, once installed, the Coventry weaver perfected the art of the jacquard ribbons so beautifully that they rivalled those from Lyons and St.Etienne. The Jacquard loom was capable of the most complicated designs and was suitable for the reproduction of black and white photographs and engravings. Many souvenir pictures were made and sold at exhibitions and important events.

The whimsical ways of fashion and world events have always influenced the ribbon industry and made it unstable. At the beginning of the nineteenth century a well-dressed French woman's ensemble could include more than fifty metres of silk ribbon – most of this would be adorning her hat! But in 1860, with the sudden frivolous preference for feathers and velvet instead of the beautiful beribboned millinery which used up to ten metres to decorate each hat, the ribbon industry began to experience a decline. Added to this, the price of silk rose because of the war in China and also the failure of the European and Indian silkworm crop. Finally, a commercial treaty with France in 1860 established free trade, resulting in French ribbons being imported at a cheaper price. All these factors caused the industry to collapse in 1860, resulting in great hardship to many thousands of weavers and their families. Many skilled weavers emigrated to the USA, Canada, Australia and New Zealand.

Following this collapse in 1860, Thomas Steven, who was determined to keep his workers in employment, used his experiments to produce pictures and bookmarks that would appeal to all tastes. By keeping his prices as low as possible, he managed to arouse enough interest and create enough demand

to keep his workers busy. He started by selling his pictures and bookmarks on barrows in the market place. They soon became well known and were then framed and sold in shops. These are now collectors' pieces. Many other manufacturers copied the idea of the Stevengraphs to see them out of the depression, but the name Thomas Steven (1828–1888) has always been closely associated with this work.

No matter how far back one goes in the history of fashion, ribbon has played its part, but never more strongly than in the fashions of the nineteenth century. The Victorians were great embroiderers and used ribbon for embroidering dresses, blouses, coats, infants' pelisses, children's dresses and coats, as well as picture frames and firescreens. There is very little authentic information as to the origin of the embroidery, but it seems it was first introduced from China via the East India Company in 1860. In fact, in Queen Anne's reign, silk was imported in large quantities and in its path appeared the dainty China ribbons. The oldest exhibited specimens of ribbon embroidery worked in this country are said to be mid-eighteenth century. After enjoying long-term popularity, it waned for a while, to be revived at the beginning of the nineteenth century.

Ribbon quilts were also made; they were the English version of the log cabin patchwork quilts of North America and were made during the last quarter of the nineteenth century from ribbons used for hat trimmings.

Boot top bands were also very fashionable in Victorian times, when ladies wore high-legged button boots reaching to the knee. Inside the boot was a two to three inch satin band woven in a jacquard design. These were very expensive to produce, but formed the backbone of one Coventry business for many years.

It was not in fact until the sixteenth century that ribbons in the present form are seen and heard of, and only in the seventeenth century that they acquired the fascination which has lasted through to the imaginative uses of today's fashionable, easy-care ribbons.

Basic Principles

Tools and equipment for ribbon weaving

- You will need a firm, flat padded surface measuring roughly 59cm × 44cm (23" × 17"). A cork board is ideal as it is light, easy to handle and enables the pins to penetrate the cork to anchor the ribbons. This board must be covered with a double layer of cotton or polycotton fabric to stop the colour from the cork damaging your ribbons when you press them.

- Glass-headed pins – these are kinder to your fingers than the normal dressmaker's pins. Although the ordinary dressmaker pin is quite alright to use, do not use the plastic-headed pin as this could melt under the heat of the iron.

- The lightest weight iron-on interfacing to bond ribbons together, making weaving easy to handle. Vilene Ultrasoft is ideal.

- A pair of sharp, medium-size scissors.

- Rouleau and loop turner for pulling ribbons through the weaving. The rouleau and loop turner is an extremely useful gadget for

weaving ribbons quickly. To use it, simply weave the rouleau and loop turner through the ribbons, place the ribbon on to the hook, close the latch pin, and pull the ribbon through the weaving. This method is far quicker and much easier than using your fingers.

- Trimming and tapemaker to make fabric trimming.
- Tape measure.
- Single- or double-faced satin ribbons. The single-faced satin is lighter in weight and is easier to handle for the weaving.
- Rotary cutter and mat.

Design and colour

For everyone who sews, the ribbon and fabric departments of any store are an Aladdin's cave of wonderful treasures. Inspiration for design and colour usually begins here with the sheer delight we feel as we dive our hands into the wealth of textures in exotic colours. It transports us momentarily to the realms of fantasy, as we visualise ourselves in a dozen different outfits embellished with ribbons and trims in numerous ways. But choosing the right fabrics, colours, ribbons and trimmings is an art in itself. To the talented few it seems an inborn skill, but to those who find it more daunting I have outlined a few simple guidelines for you to follow.

- Never be afraid of colour, choose the colours you like best and follow your own instincts. You will soon develop a more adventurous sense of colour as your design sense also grows. Colour is vital in our lives and affects everything we do – the way we respond to our surroundings and to other people – so it is important to make the right choices.
- If you have a favourite colour try mixing fabrics and ribbons entirely in tones of this colour (monotone schemes). The effect will be very elegant and looks beautiful especially if soft pastel shades are used. When used in furnishings this scheme creates a Scandinavian look.
- Rich, strong dark colours look dramatic warm and inviting but do make sure your background fabric is equally as strong. These colours look good in old houses with oak beams.
- For an antique or muted look choose soft grey dusty tones. Keep the colours muted by using a soft background in velvets, silk taffeta and moiré.

Whichever colours you favour, one failsafe tip when choosing the ribbons for your cushions or fashion garments is to use one ribbon that matches as closely as possible the background fabric you will be using. This one vital factor will give your weaving and embroidery a look of being an integral part of the garment or your furnishing scheme. For excitingly rich texture try weaving fabric with ribbon, either in the same colours or using contrasts, and vary the widths.

Fabrics

When choosing your background fabric for fashion or soft furnishing look carefully at it before buying: does it have a pattern on it that will be destroyed by cutting and seaming? As you will be adding a lot of surface decoration with ribbon weaving or embroidery it is better to use plain fabrics with an interesting texture as the ribbon work itself will create a rich and exciting surface decoration. Have your background fabric with you when choosing your ribbons as colour is very difficult to remember. Place the ribbons onto the fabric and you will see immediately which colours look good with your fabric and which to discard. The same principle applies for your cushions – find one ribbon to match the fabric and place the other colours around it until you are happy with your choice whichever colour scheme you have chosen to work in.

It is most important to use good quality fabrics for your garments or furnishings. Do check that they will wash and wear well, or dry clean, as a lot of work will go into your weaving and appliqué and the making up of garments and cushions.

Choosing your ribbons

It is very important to choose the right ribbon for the work in hand. There are basically two types of ribbon – **woven edge** and **cut edge**.

Cut-edge ribbons

Cut-edge ribbons are used for craft work and floral work. They are made from large rolls of fabric cut into lengthways strips to the desired width, but before cutting, these fabrics are treated with a special sizing to add crispness to stop the fabric from fraying. It is because of this special finish that craft ribbons are not suitable for any fashion garments or soft furnishings, as they are not normally washable or dry cleanable.

Woven-edge ribbons

The ribbons used in this book are woven-edge ribbons. These are essentially narrow pieces of fabric with two selvedge edges and can be washed or dry cleaned. All the ribbons used for fashion and furnishings must be woven-edge ribbons. For the work I will be showing you, single-faced satin ribbons (shiny on one side only) are ideal for all ribbon weaving and appliqué work, as they are soft and pliable and lighter in weight than the double-faced satin ribbon (shiny on both sides). The latter are used mainly for streamers and bows where both sides of the ribbon will show. For all the designs in this book you can use either single- or double-faced satin ribbons – the choice is yours.

Grosgrain ribbons
Grosgrain ribbons are available in a wide range of solid colours and patterns, and are very distinctive by their crosswise rib. One particular grosgrain ribbon has a very distinctive picot edge and because it is so crisp and stable it will keep its shape beautifully. It makes a perfect trimming for soft furnishing (table cloths, mats and cushions for example) and can also be used for special effects and pleated into fan shapes on hat boxes. This ribbon is usually dry clean only.

Jacquard ribbons
Jacquard ribbons are richly woven ribbons in beautiful patterns. In the majority of jacquards the colours are laid out in the warp ribbons, with the weft ribbon woven in one colour making the backs of these ribbons as colourful and interesting as the right side. The designs on the jacquards are many and varied, and add wonderful colour and texture when used as a trimming on both fashion and home furnishing, and for children's wear.

Velvet nylon ribbons
Velvet nylon ribbons are produced in rich jewel colours as well as soft pastel shades, and have a plush pile surface. They are very hard wearing and washable, and when used in contrast with satins or jacquards make interesting opulent textures.

Sheer ribbons
Sheer ribbons are plain or printed, and are often woven with metallic or satin stripes or spots. Many are made with an extra monofilament along one edge that serves as a pull cord for gathering the ribbon. They create light airy embellishment and make lovely ribbon roses that glisten and gleam in the evening lights.

Metallic ribbons
Metallic ribbons are made from Lurex fibres or are interwoven with other fibres. They glisten brightly and look beautiful when used on evening wear. They look fabulous mixed with satin ribbon or with fabric weaving.

Taffeta ribbons
Taffeta ribbons are woven in a large variety of colours and designs – ginghams and plaids being the most popular. Because the design is woven in, these ribbons appear the same on both sides. The design and colour of the plaid ribbon is in the warp threads, with one colour being used to weave across the weft (the same as the jacquard ribbon). Ideal for making bows, especially when wire edged.

The ideal choice for all your fashion and home furnishings are the easy-care polyester satins, the nylon velvets and the woven boil-proof jacquards or the petersham ribbons. All these ribbons will have a long and useful life and will hopefully be passed down to the next generation as family heirlooms, so a lot of thought and care must go into your choice of ribbons. The sheer and metallic ribbons are lovely used for accessories.

To create interesting textures, weave wide and narrow ribbons together to create a quilted look, or try mixing the beautiful jacquard ribbons with velvets or satins. The polyester grosgrain ribbon is ideal for belts and purses, either woven together or used as an edging and top stitched in place as a decorative trim. Working with ribbons of one colour but using various textures and widths can look very elegant.

Ribbon Weaving Techniques

Plain weave

This is the simplest form of ribbon weaving and like other methods of weaving, consists of interlocking warp threads (vertical) with weft threads (horizontal), except that ribbon is used instead of yarns to create your own individual fabric. Many different patterns can be created by using various weaving sequences, and a whole range of patterns and textures can be made by mixing various widths of ribbon, lace or broderie anglaise and fabric.

The whole process is made very easy by weaving the ribbons over lightweight iron-on interfacing and, using a warm steam iron and damp cloth, bonding the woven ribbons into fabric which makes it easy to handle. It is ideal for cutting out shapes and incorporating into either fashion garments, furnishing accessories or craft ideas.

Beautiful cushions with the accents on colour, texture and techniques will help to co-ordinate your furnishing scheme and make your room look complete. The lovely cushion featured here has a centre panel of ribbon weaving, trimmed with bands of petersham ribbon and decorative cord, and edged with a luxurious fringe. It is very easy to make and requires only the simple plain weave for the centre of the cushion and the ability to machine in a straight line when applying the petersham ribbon. Once you have mastered this simple technique you will soon discover a wealth of ideas of your own. Try using a variety of different weaves for the centre of additional cushions, using colours that pick out and heighten secondary colours in the room, or maybe you would prefer to use strong

colours that provide a striking contrast. Whatever your choice of colour and texture, beautiful cushions provide a really warm, luxurious and very practical addition to your room.

Helpful tip

To make your cushions look nice and plump, always cut your fabric to the same size as your cushion pad. This will give a really snug fit, plumping up the cushions and enhancing any decorative work you may wish to add.

The following instructions are for an 18cm (7") square of ribbon weaving for the centre panel of a cushion – an ideal way to start.

Materials

- Cut two sections of fabric measuring 38cm (15") square (35.5cm /14" cushion)
- 1.70 metres (1yd 27") petersham ribbon, 36mm (1½") wide in Linden green
- 4 metres (4½yd) double-faced satin ribbon, 3mm (⅛") wide in Linden green
- 4 metres (4½yd) single-faced satin ribbon, 13mm (½") wide in peach
- 1.60 metres (1yd 24") matching decorative cord trim
- 2 metres (2½yd) decorative fringe trimming for the edge of the cushion
- 18cm (7") square of Vilene Ultrasoft iron-on interfacing
- Matching thread to the petersham ribbon for top stitching
- 1 cork board covered in a polycotton (for working the ribbon weaving) – a cork tile will do
- Glass-headed pins
- 18cm (7") zip (optional extra)

Method – ribbon weaving for cushion centre: plain weave using two widths and two colours

Warp ribbons
Place interfacing adhesive side up onto the cork board.

Mark grain lines straight down centre of square and across centre of square.

Cut the 13mm (½") wide ribbon and the 3mm (⅛") wide ribbon into 11 lengths measuring 18cm (7"), using the two widths and colours for the warp ribbons and the two widths and colours for the weft ribbons.

Place the first warp ribbon down the centre of the grain line and pin firmly top and bottom, making sure the ribbon is firmly anchored. Pin out the remaining warp ribbons side by side, edges together, using the wide and narrow ribbons alternately, until the interfacing is covered.

Weft ribbons

Weave the first weft ribbon across the centre grain line, weaving under one, over one, under one to the end of the row. Pin the ribbon firmly in place.

Weave the second row, over one, under one over one to the end of the row.

Now weave the either side of the grain line ribbon until the weft ribbons are complete and the interfacing is completely covered (Fig 1), using the green and peach ribbon alternately.

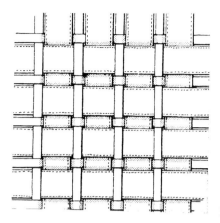

Fig 1

Finishing

When the weaving is complete, place a dry muslin cloth over the ribbon weaving and pins, carefully remove one row of pins making sure the ribbons do not move.

Using a steam iron, gently press the ribbons through the dry cloth, carefully removing the rest of the pins as you press to bond the ribbons to the interfacing.

Turn the weaving to the reverse side and press again, this time use a damp cloth to press the ribbons well and bond to the interfacing

When this is complete, trim around the edge of the ribbon weaving to neaten it, and machine 1cm in from the edge of the weaving to hold the ribbons in position

Press.

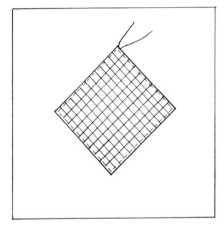

Fig 2

Making up the cushion

Place the square of weaving in the centre of your cushion panel following the diagram (Fig 2). Machine in position and press carefully.

Place the first band of petersham ribbon across the top and bottom of the woven panel, covering the raw edges by 1cm. Machine the petersham ribbon in place by top stitching close to the edge of the ribbon. Press carefully.

To apply the cord trim to the edge of the remaining petersham ribbon, simply place it along

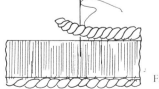

Fig 3

the edge of the ribbon and stitch through the cord and the ribbon with very loose stitches (Fig 3). Place the corded petersham ribbon each side of the woven panel and over the first petersham ribbons, covering the edges of the weaving again by 1cm. Top stitch in position (Fig 4). When this corded ribbon is machined in place, the decorative cord can then be rolled onto the edge of the petersham ribbon to hide your machine stitching.

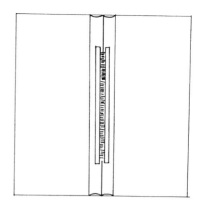

Fig 5

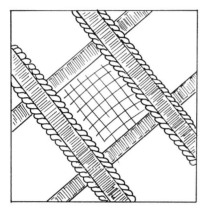

Fig 4

Place the fringing around the edge of the cushion, over the decorative work, loose fringes facing towards the centre of the cushion, making sure the corners are nice and full. Machine in place.

For the zip (optional extra), you will need two sections of fabric for the back of your cushion measuring 38cm × 21cm = 2cm seam down the centre back (15" × 8"). With the right sides of the fabric together, pin and machine the top and base of the centre back section together to a depth of 10cm (4"). Press seams open. Tack the zip in place centrally over the seam and between the machine stitching. Machine stitch all around the zip (Fig 5).

Place the back panel of the cushion over the ribbon work and fringing, pin and tack in position.

Machine stitch in place by following the row of stitches used to stitch the fringing in position, machine around the four sides leaving an 20cm (8") gap on one side of the cushion. (Note: if a zip is used in the centre back panel leave it open when machining the back and front together and machine all around the four sides, turn the cushion through the open zip.) Turn the cushion to the right side through the gap, making sure the fringed corners are neat and full. Turn in seam allowance along back edge and slip-stitch the seam together.

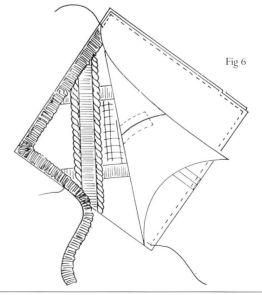

Fig 6

Bias weave

This is a most versatile weave and can be made to look different every time you weave it, by simply using various widths of ribbon, or by the way in which you weave together two different colours. Weaving one colour for the warp and another colour for the weft will give you a checker-board weave, but if you weave the two colours alternately across both warp and weft, you will weave the fabric into a stripe like the centre of this lovely cushion.

The finished measurements of the panel below are 18cm × 48cm (7" × 19").

Materials for the cushion panel

- 10 metres (11yd) double-faced satin ribbon, 3mm (⅛") wide in soft green
- 10 metres (11yd) single-faced satin ribbon, 13mm (½") wide in peach
- 1 metre (1¼yd) petersham ribbon, 36mm (1½") wide in soft green
- 4 metres of matching decorative cord trim
- 2.20 metres (2yd 17") of decorative fringe trimming for the edge of the cushion
- 2 × 49cm (19¼") squares of furnishing fabric for the cushion
- Vilene Ultrasoft iron-on interfacing, 19cm × 49cm (7¾" × 19½")
- Glass-headed pins
- Matching thread to the petersham ribbon for top stitching
- 1 cork board covered in a double layer of polycotton for working the ribbon weaving

Method – ribbon weaving for cushion centre:
bias weave using two widths and two colours

Warp ribbons
Place the interfacing adhesive side up onto your covered cork board.

Fold the interfacing on the diagonal to mark your bias centre, and mark with a marker pen.

Place the first warp ribbon along this centre line, cut the ribbon to fit the interfacing and pin firmly in place.

Place the second warp ribbon on the right-hand side of the centre ribbon, cut to fit interfacing.

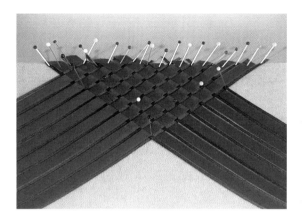

Continue to place the ribbons side by side until the interfacing is covered, making sure all ribbons are close together (Fig 1). Continue to cut and pin down the warp ribbons on the left-hand side of the centre line, until the interfacing is completely covered (alternating one peach ribbon and one green ribbon).

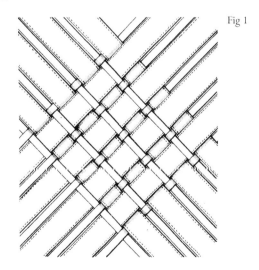

Fig 1

Weft ribbons

Starting again in the bias centre (not in the corner) with your 3mm (⅛") wide ribbon, weave the ribbon under one, over one, until the row is complete.

Weave the second weft ribbon (13mm/½" wide ribbon), over one, under one, to the end of the row, keeping it close to the first ribbon and working on the right-hand side of the centre until this part is complete. Weave the left-hand section in the same way until the weaving is completed (alternating one green one peach ribbon). To keep ribbons taut and straight, place a few pins along the centre of the first weft ribbon; these can be moved along as the work progresses.

Finishing

When the weaving is complete, place a dry muslin cloth over the ribbons and pins and carefully remove the row of pins from the top edge, making sure the ribbons do not move.

Using a steam iron, gently press the ribbons over your dry cloth, close to the pins, removing the pins carefully as you press.

Turn the weaving to the reverse side and this time using a damp cloth, press well to bond the ribbon weaving to the interfacing.

Trim around the edge of your ribbon weaving to measure 18cm × 50cm (7" × 20"). Machine stitch all around the edge of your cut out section 1cm (⅜") in from the edge. This eliminates any movement of the ribbons, and your weaving is now ready to use in your cushion.

Making up the cushion

Place your woven panel centrally on to the cushion square, machine panel in position (Fig 2) and press carefully from the wrong side.

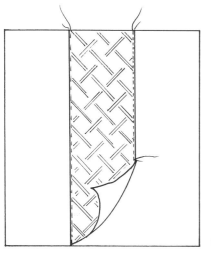

Fig 2

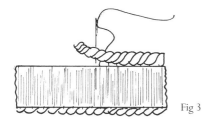

Fig 3

Apply the cord trim to the petersham ribbon (Fig 3) by placing the cord along the edge of the petersham ribbon and stitching it very loosely to the edge of the ribbon. Press ribbon very carefully when finished.

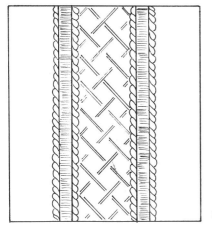

Fig 4

Place the corded petersham ribbon each side of the woven centre panel covering the raw edges of the weaving by 1cm (⅜") (Fig 4). Machine in place by using the cording foot on your sewing machine – you will find you can roll the cord out of the way while you machine the ribbon in position. The decorative cord can then be rolled on to the edge of the petersham ribbon to hide your machine stitching. Alternatively the cord trim could be sewn in place after the petersham ribbon is machined in place.

Place the fringed trim around the edge of the cushion, over the decorative work, loose fringes facing towards the centre of the cushion, and make sure the corners are full (Fig 5). Machine fringing in place. (Join fringing along side of cushion away from the ribbon work.)

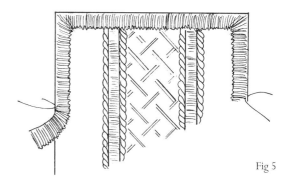

Fig 5

Place the back panel of the cushion over the ribbon work and fringing, right sides facing, pin and tack in position. Machine stitch in place by following the row of stitches used to machine the fringing in place. Machine stitch around the four sides leaving open a gap of 20cm (8") on one side of the cushion.

Turn the cushion to the right side through the gap, making sure fringed corners are neat and full,

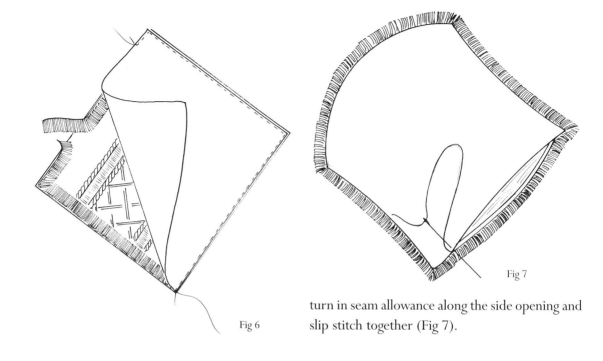

Fig 6

turn in seam allowance along the side opening and slip stitch together (Fig 7).

Fig 7

Zig-zag weave

This is a very unusual weave and when it is woven with various widths of ribbon it looks very attractive. The zig-zag design is a four row pattern, the fifth row being the same as the first row, weaving under and over two ribbons but stepping down one ribbon as you weave. It is ideal used for the centre of a cushion woven in narrow ribbons, using either contrasting colours or woven in ribbons of one colour. In the diagram below two colours were used in this weave with ribbons of the same width, but the cushion I designed was made with using two widths of ribbon. This design looks stunning woven in black and white and made into an evening purse.

Materials for cushion 41cm (16") square

- 4 metres (4¼yd) single- or double-faced satin ribbon, 10mm (⅜") in two colours
- 1.30cm (1½yd) picot-edged petersham ribbon, 56mm (2") wide
- 1.80cm (2yd) decorative cord trim
- Vilene Ultrasoft iron-on interfacing 20cm (8") square
- Glass-headed pins
- Covered cork board
- 41cm (16") cushion pad
- Fabric for cushion, two squares 41cm (16")

Method

Place the iron-on interfacing on your cork board adhesive side up. Mark your centre grain line for the warp and weft ribbons.

Starting from the centre grain line, pin down an odd number of warp ribbons until your interfacing is covered. If two colours are used, begin and end with the same colour ribbon.

To weave weft ribbons, alternate colour A and B as follows:

For this pattern only, it is easier to start at the top right-hand corner.

Row one: Colour A, under two, over two, to the end of the row.

Row two: Colour B, under one, then over two, under two, over two. Repeat to the end.

Row three: Colour A, over two, under two, over two. Repeat to the end.

Row four: Colour B, over one, then under two, over two, under two. Repeat to the end.

These four rows form the zig-zag pattern. Continue to weave rows 1 to 4 until the weaving is complete.

Finishing

When the weaving is complete press gently with a dry cloth over the pins, remove pins carefully and press again on the back with a damp cloth to bond the ribbons well

Trim weaving to size 18cm (7") square, machine around edge 1cm (⅜") in from edge.

Press well.

Making up

Place your woven panel in the centre of your fabric square and machine in place (Fig 2).

Fig 1

1st row

2nd row

3rd row

4th row

Fig 2

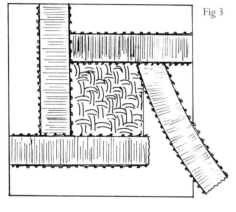

Fig 3

Following the diagram in Fig 3, place the first petersham ribbon over the raw edges of the woven panel, keeping the raw edge of the petersham ribbon in line with the woven panel. Machine in place on the outside edge only. Position the second ribbon in place under the first petersham, covering the edges of the woven panel again. Stitch again along the outside edge only. Continue to place the ribbons in position following the diagram in Fig 3. When all these ribbons are in place, machine the inner edge of petersham ribbon to complete the design, keeping ribbons firmly in place. Press carefully over the machine stitching.

Place the back panel over the front panel, right sides facing (Fig 4) and machine together leaving part of one side section open to turn cushion through to the right side. Hand stitch sides seam together.

Trim the cushion with decorative cord trimming and four large tassels (Fig 5).

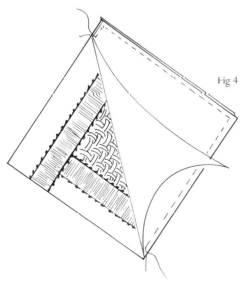

Fig 4

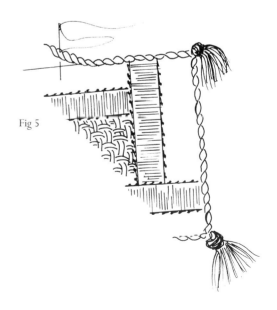

Fig 5

Cube weave

This fascinating cushion will enhance any furnishing scheme it is placed in, and will delight everyone who sees it. Friends will also marvel at your new found skill. As you can see, this is not the easiest design to weave, but I'm sure you will agree it is worth the extra effort of working it out. The inspiration for this cube weave, or tumbling blocks design, originated from the American patchwork worked at the turn of the century.

The depth of the design is achieved by using three different shades of ribbon – a light, medium and dark. In this cushion the light ribbon is gold, the medium ribbon is the red Swiss jacquard and the dark ribbon is bottle green. This three-dimensional weave is woven in triple weaving, creating a cube pattern and is produced by using one warp ribbon (the gold) and two weft ribbons (the red jacquard and the bottle green).

Materials for cushion 41cm (16") square

- ☞ 2 metres 20cm (2½yd) single- or double-faced satin, 22mm (3/4") wide in gold
- ☞ 2 metres 30cm (2½yd) single- or double-faced satin, 22mm (¾") wide in dark green
- ☞ 2 metres 30cm (2½yd) Swiss jacquard ribbon, 22mm (¾") wide in red
- ☞ 1 metre 40cm (1yd 33") picot-edged petersham ribbon in red
- ☞ A piece of Vilene Ultrasoft iron-on

- interfacing 22cm (8½") square
- ☞ Two pieces of furnishing fabric 42cm (16½") square
- ☞ 1 metre 70cm (1yd 31")of contrasting fringing
- ☞ Glass headed pins
- ☞ Cork board covered in polycotton fabric to protect the ribbons when pressing
- ☞ A cushion pad measuring 43cm (17")

In this design, the warp consists of lengthways strips of ribbon, with two sets of weft ribbons, one woven diagonally across the warp from the top left-hand corner, and the other set from the right-hand corner.

This produces your patchwork pattern, and a material of three thicknesses. It is therefore, very hard wearing, ideal for cushions and grows very quickly because the ribbons are quite wide.

Method

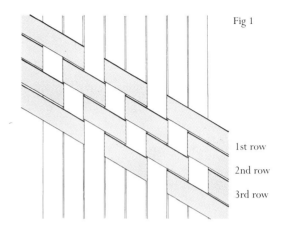

Fig 1

1st row
2nd row
3rd row

Warp ribbons (light-coloured ribbon)
Place the interfacing adhesive side up on to the cork board.

Cut 10 lengths of the gold ribbon 22cm (8½") long, and pin them side by side, edges touching, until the interfacing is covered. Make sure you pin them securely at the top and bottom (Fig 1).

First weft (dark green ribbon)
Weave diagonally from the right-hand side, weaving this first ribbon from approximately one-third of the way up from the bottom right-hand corner (Fig 1).

Row one: *over two, under one, over two*, repeat to the end.

Row two: over one, *under one, over two, under one*, repeat from * to *.

Row three: *under one, over two*, repeat from * to *.

Repeat this three-row pattern to the bottom left-hand corner, cutting the ribbon and pinning down as you work. The cut ribbons can be used on the opposite side with no further cutting, avoiding waste.

Now complete the weaving by working towards the top right-hand corner.

Second weft (jacquard ribbon)
When working the second weft ribbon, a few of the pins already placed around the edge will need to be removed and re-pinned as you weave.

Beginning at the top right-hand corner, weave diagonally across, towards the left in the following three-row pattern, weaving the first ribbon to one-third of the way up from the bottom left-hand corner.

Row one: *under two, over one*, repeat from * to *.

Row two: *over one, under two*, repeat from * to *.

Row three: under one, *over one, under two*, repeat from * to * to end of row (Fig 2).

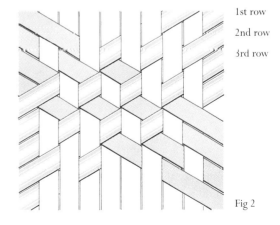

1st row
2nd row
3rd row

Fig 2

This pattern refers to weaving over and under the upright warp ribbon. The second weft, however, also passes under and over the first weft ribbon, and can only be achieved if the angle is correct. Weaving this double weft in three colours – one dark and two lighter shades – makes an interesting cube design and is well worth the effort involved.

Finishing

When the weaving is complete, place a dry muslin cloth over the ribbon weaving and pins, making sure the ribbons do not move.

Using a steam iron, gently press the ribbons through the dry cloth, carefully removing the pins as you press.

Turn the weaving to the reverse side and press again with a damp cloth to bond the ribbons to the interfacing.

Trim around the edge of the ribbon weaving to neaten it, and machine just in from the edge to hold the weaving in position.

Press.

Your weaving is now ready to use.

Making up the cushion

Following the illustrations (Figs 2 and 3) for the zig-zag weave cushion, proceed as follows:

Place your woven panel in the centre of your fabric square, roughly 10cm (4") in from each side. Machine in position.

Cut the petersham ribbon into four equal lengths and place each section over the raw edges of the woven panel following Fig 3. Press carefully.

Place the fringed trimming around the edge of the cushion, loose fringes facing towards the centre of the cushion, making sure the corners are full. Machine the fringing in place.

Place the back of the cushion over the fringed trimming, right sides together, pin in place. Machine together on all four sides leaving a 20cm (8") opening on one side of the cushion. (For accurate machining follow the machine stitching for the fringing.)

Turn the cushion to the right side through the opening making sure the corner fringing is pulled through.

Place the cushion pad in the cover and hand stitch the opening.

Alternative cushion design

As this weaving produces a hard wearing panel you may wish to use the lovely cube design on its own, without placing the woven panel onto another fabric. In this case increase the size of the weaving to 31cm (12") and follow the making up instruction diagrams Figs 3 to 8, making a covered cord trimming in your background fabric.

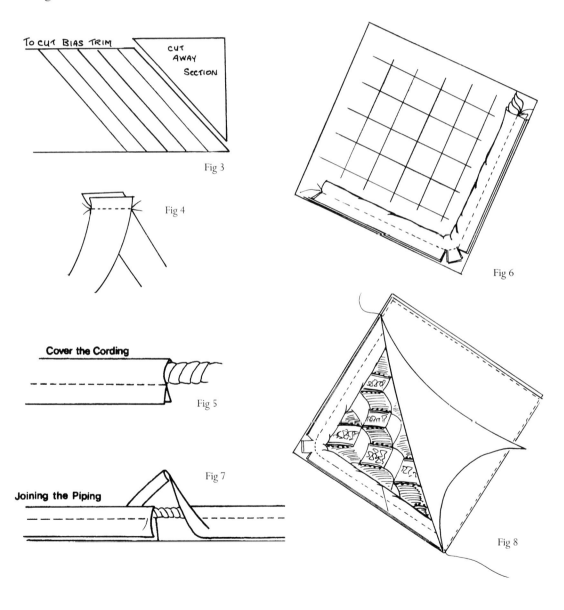

To cut Bias Trim

CUT AWAY SECTION

Fig 3

Fig 4

Fig 6

Cover the Cording

Fig 5

Fig 7

Joining the Piping

Fig 8

Fabric and Ribbon Weaving Techniques

Weaving fabric and ribbon together creates the most wonderfully colourful rich and opulent textures – it is also a very economical way of using all those lovely fabrics you could not resist buying but never found time to use. The techniques that are given here are suitable for any fabrics that can be stitched and pressed without puckering. I have used this technique on many cushions, table mats, waistcoats and wedding dresses and it always looks fabulous.

There are two methods you can use to achieve a very similar look. One method is to use a trimming and tape maker – in effect to make your own bias trimming – which I will explain later. The second method which I prefer, is to cut the fabric into strips, machine it and turn it through to the right side and press. I have used a variety of fabrics for the different projects I have worked on, but for the best results I have found silk to be the most versatile of all. The silk fabric I used for cushion I have designed and made for you here, was hand painted by Mary Day.

Silk painted cushion:
finished size – 30.5cm × 40.5cm (12" × 16")

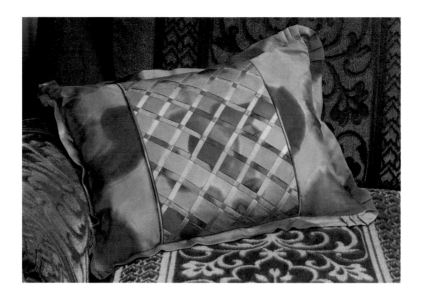

Materials required

- 1 metre (1¼yd) of silk, 112cm (44") wide
- 5 metres ((5½yd) single- or double-faced satin ribbon, 7mm (¼") wide
- Vilene Ultrasoft iron-on interfacing, 23.5cm × 33cm (9" × 13")
- 3 buttons to cover
- 1 cushion pad 40.5cm (16") square

- Matching sewing thread
- Covered cork board for the weaving
- Glass-headed pins
- 70 cm (27½") of piping cord
- The fabric used for this cushion was spun silk taffeta.

Cutting out

For the two back panels of the cushion:
- Cut one section measuring 38 cm × 33cm (15" × 13")
- Cut one section measuring 24 cm × 33 cm (9½" × 13")
- Cut two side front panels measuring 13cm × 33cm (5¼" × 13")
- Cut 10 strips of fabric measuring 6.5cm (2½") wide by the width of the fabric (cut across the fabric on the straight grain = 112cm / 44")

Method

Warp ribbons

Fold five of the 6.5 cm (2½") wide strips of fabric in half lengthways right sides together. Machine 1 cm (⅜") in from the raw edges (Fig 3). Turn the strips through to the right sides and press flat with the seam running along the one side, not in the middle.

Place your interfacing onto the covered cork board adhesive side facing you. Mark your bias centre with a marker pen.

Take the first fabric strip and place it along it on this centre line. Trim the fabric strip to fit your interfacing. Pin firmly in place (Fig 1).

Fig 3

Place the second warp ribbon (ribbon) on the right-hand side of the fabric strip, trim it to fit the interfacing, pin firmly in place. Continue to place the ribbons and fabric strips alternating, side by side, until the interfacing is covered, making sure the ribbons and fabric are close together with the edges touching. Continue to cut and pin down the warp ribbons on the left-hand side of the centre line, until the interfacing is completely covered (alternating one ribbon and one fabric strip).

Weft ribbons

Starting again in the bias centre with your ribbon (not in the top corner), weave the ribbon under one, over one, until the row is complete (Fig 2).

Weave the second weft ribbon (fabric strip) over one, under one, to the end of the row, keeping it close to the ribbon and working on the right-hand side of this centre ribbon until this part of the weaving is complete. Weave the left-hand section in the same way until the weaving is completed (alternating one fabric strip and one ribbon).

To keep ribbons taut and straight, place a few pins along the centre of the first weft ribbon; these can be moved along as the work progresses.

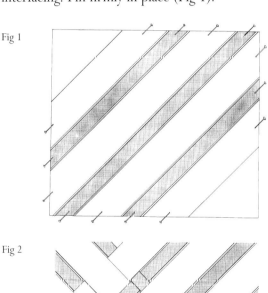

Fig 1

Fig 2

Finishing

When the weaving is complete, place a dry muslin cloth over the weaving and the pins. Carefully remove the row of pins from the top edge, making sure the ribbons do not move.

Using a steam iron, gently press the weaving over your dry cloth, close to the pins removing the pins carefully as you press.

Turn the weaving to the reverse side and this time using a damp cloth, press well to bond the weaving to the interfacing.

Trim around the edge of your ribbon weaving to measure 26cm × 15cm (10¼" × 6")

Machine stitch all around the edge of your cut out section 0.5cm (¼") in from the edge. This eliminates any movement of the ribbons and fabric, and your weaving is now ready to use in your cushion.

Making up

Take one of the fabric strips and cover the piping cord (Fig 4). Machine in place with a cording foot, close to the piping. Cut the cord in half.

Fig 4

Place one piece of the covered piping cord over the seam allowance on the woven section, along the shorter side, raw edges together. Machine in place (Fig 5).

Pin the side panels to the woven panel over the piping cord and machine in place. Following the

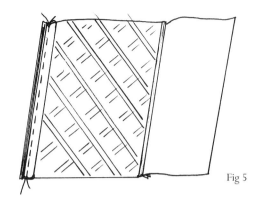

Fig 5

machine stitches for the piping cord helps with accuracy of stitching. Press all seams towards the side seam. To open out this seam would create too much bulk because of the woven section.

Cushion frill

You will need three lengths of the fabric strips seamed together across the width of the strip, to make the long frill for the cushion.

Machine seam together and press open.

Fold strip in half lengthways and press carefully along the length of the strip.

Pin folded strip carefully in position all around the front cushion panel edge, pleating three pleats into the corner and three pleats out of each of the four corners of the cushion. Make sure the folded edge is facing the centre of the cushion, raw edges together.

Machine in place 1cm (⅜") in from raw edges.

Press machine stitching.

Back panels

The back panel is in two sections. On the larger panel along the shorter edge, fold back 10cm (4"), then fold this double reducing to 5cm (2").

Do the same with the second panel folding back 8cm (3"), reducing again to 4cm (1½").

Make three covered buttons.

Make three button holes in the largest panel.

Stitch buttons in place and fasten together. Check the back panel now measures the same as the front panel, 33cm × 43cm (13" × 17") (Fig 6).

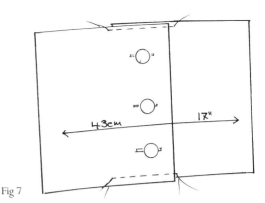

Fig 7

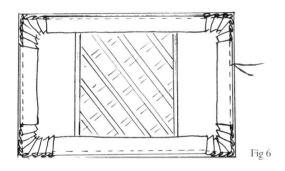

Fig 6

With right sides facing, place the front panels over the back panels, pin and machine in place (Fig 7).

Press machine stitching.

Trim corners, turn through to right side through the button opening.

A 40.5cm (16") cushion pad was then made to

Fig 8

fit into this cushion which gives it that lovely firm plumped-up look (see below for making up a cushion pad).

Ring cushion

A ring cushion for the bride and groom carried by the page boys is such a lovely idea for a wedding, and with this cushion design the rings will not fall to the floor. I designed and made this lovely ring cushion for the wedding of my youngest son, Paul, to Louise. It was carried by the two page boys (my two grand-sons). The fabric used was purple and ivory silk dupion with the fabric and ribbon woven centre panel, trimmed with gold and purple cord and four large gold tassels.

Materials required

- 40cm (½yd) pure silk dupion in purple
- Two sections of ivory silk dupion, 26cm × 12.5cm (10¼" × 5")
- 3 metres (3¼yd) double-faced satin ribbon, 6mm (¼") wide
- 1 section of Vilene Ultrasoft iron-on interfacing measuring 26cm × 16cm (10¼" × 6¼")
- 2 metres (2¼yd) of decorative cord trim
- 4 large tassels
- A cork board covered in a double layer of polycotton, for the weaving
- Glass-headed pins
- Thread to match the purple fabric

Materials for the cushion pad

- Two sections of calico measuring 34cm × 26cm (13½" × 10¼"), 1cm (⅜") seam allowance.
- Enough kapok to fill the cushion pad, making it a good shape.

Making up the pad

Make up the calico cushion pad by placing the two pieces of calico, right sides together and machine around three sides leaving one short side open.

Trim seams.

Turn through to the right side and press.

Fill the cushion pad with kapok.

Hand or machine stitch the open edges together.

Open out flat the purple dupion fabric and cut two sections measuring 35cm × 26cm (14" × 10¼") – this allows for a 1.5cm (⅝") seam all around.

Fold the remaining fabric on the bias and cut into strips of fabric measuring 6.5cm (2½") wide.

Fold these strips in half lengthways and machine with right sides together 1cm (⅜") from the edges.

Turn the bias strips through to the right side and press flat with the seam running along one side. Be careful not to stretch them.

Fabric and ribbon weaving

Warp ribbons
Place the interfacing onto your covered cork, board adhesive side facing you. Mark the bias grain with a marker pen.

Take the first fabric strip and place it along it on this centre line (warp ribbon). Cut the fabric strip to fit the interfacing (Fig 1). Pin firmly in place but do not stretch.

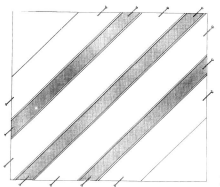

Fig 1

Place the second warp ribbon (ivory ribbon) on the right-hand side of the fabric strip, cut it to fit the interfacing and pin firmly in place. Continue to place the ribbons and fabric strips alternating, side by side, until the interfacing is covered, making sure the ribbons and fabric are close together, the edges touching. Continue to cut and pin down the warp ribbons on the left-hand side of the centre line, until the interfacing is completely covered (alternating one ivory ribbon and one purple fabric strip).

Weft ribbons
Starting again in the bias centre with your ivory ribbon (not in the top corner), weave the ribbon under one, over one, until the row is complete (Fig 2).

Fig 2

Weave the second weft ribbon (fabric strip) over one, under one, to the end of the row, keeping it close to the ivory ribbon and working on the right-hand side of this centre ribbon until this part of the weaving is complete. Weave the left-hand section in the same way until the weaving is completed (alternating one fabric strip and one ivory ribbon).

To keep ribbons taut and straight, place a few pins along the centre of the first weft ribbon; these can be moved along as the work progresses.

Finishing

When the weaving is complete, place a dry muslin cloth over the weaving and pins. Carefully remove the row of pins from the top edge, making sure the ribbons do not move.

Using a steam iron, gently press the weaving over your dry cloth close to the pins, removing the pins carefully as you press.

Turn the weaving to the reverse side and this time using a damp cloth, press well to bond the weaving to the interfacing.

Trim around the edge of your ribbon weaving to measure 26cm × 15cm (10¼" × 6").

Machine stitch all around the edge of your

cut-out section, 0.5cm (¼") in from the edge. This eliminates any movement of the ribbons and fabric, and your weaving is now ready to use in your cushion.

Making up

Pin side panels of ivory dupion to the woven panel (Fig 3) and machine in place. Press all seams towards side seams (to open out this seam would create too much bulk because of the weaving).

Hand stitch cording in place over this seam (Fig 4).

With right sides together, place the second piece of purple dupion over the woven section, pin and

Fig 3

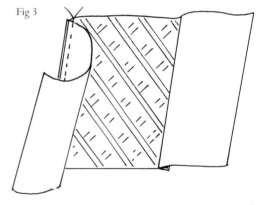

Fig 4

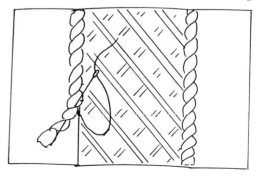

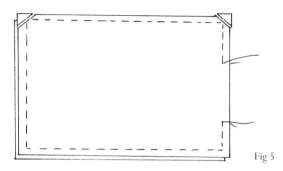

Fig 5

machine in place leaving a section open (Fig 5). Press the machine stitches. Turn through to the right side.

Place the calico cushion pad inside the cushion sham and hand stitch the open edges.

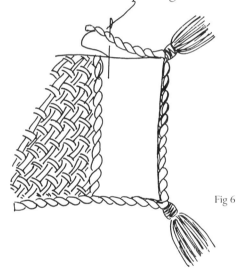

Fig 6

Place the decorative cord trim around the edge of the cushion and hand stitch in position. Tuck the raw ends into the hand-stitched side panel.

Add the four golden tassels, one to each corner of the ring cushion (Fig 6).

The rings are then tied in place with separate lengths of ribbon through the woven panel.

Wire-edged rose

Ribbon Roses

An easy and pretty way to add a touch of haute couture – a designer's signature – to your garments is with ribbon or fabric roses, using the same fabric as the dress itself with matching or contrasting ribbon. This simple detail can lift a dress, jacket or evening gown out of the ordinary into the unique, giving it your own individual look. Try using clusters of roses to cascade down the backs of evening gowns, at the waist of jackets or on a lapel. Place them on special occasion shoes (see page 89 for wedding shoes) or dotted over a waistcoat – the variations are endless. Use several fabrics and ribbons combined together: organza for light, airy roses, taffeta for a stiffer rose or satins for large glossy roses like the those illustrated on the cover of the book. Once you have learned the various techniques of rose making you will find endless uses for them, from sumptuous packaging to elaborate millinery and even vases full of hand-made roses.

Folded rose

Any width of ribbon can be used to make this versatile rose and numerous qualities of ribbon can be used depending on the look you wish to achieve. The wider the ribbon the more you will need, the narrower the ribbon the less you will use. These roses are beautiful made in single-faced satin ribbon so that the shiny and dull sides show as you twist and turn the ribbon, but they are just as lovely in double-faced satin, organza, taffeta or wire-edged ribbon depending on the look you are trying to achieve.

Method

You will need approximately 40cm (16") of ribbon, 35mm wide (1¼") ribbon to make one rose.

Place the ribbon in your right hand. right sides facing you. Fold the end of the ribbon to form an angle of 45 degrees (Fig 1).

Holding the ribbon with the right hand, twist the ribbon firmly backwards with the left hand to form a tight roll, until all the diagonal line is used up (Figs 2 and 3). This will form the stem of the rose.

Place the stem in your left hand, take the loose ribbon in your right hand, lift the ribbon upwards folding it over at the top edge, keeping it level, at the same time twisting with the left hand, clockwise (Fig 4).

The centre, which is tight, will now start to open out, forming the centre of the rose (Fig 5). Repeat Fig 4, three times.

Now place the rose between the first and second finger of the right hand, with the centre facing you (Fig 6). Now fold the ribbon backwards and place

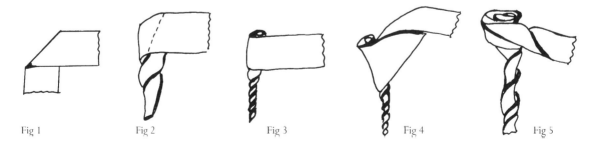

Fig 1 Fig 2 Fig 3 Fig 4 Fig 5

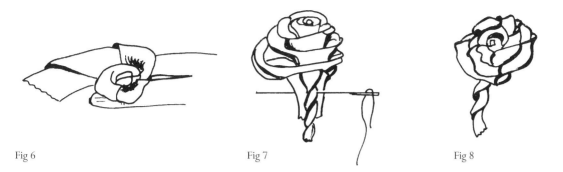

Fig 6   Fig 7   Fig 8

the ribbon under the rose while turning the rose clockwise. Gently place your thumb over the centre of the rosebud while turning it clockwise.

When the desired size is reached, place the end of the ribbon along the stem of the rose and stitch to keep it firmly in place (Figs 7 and 8).

Concertina rose

This particular rose can be made with a wide or narrow ribbon or with a wire edge. The double-faced satins are quite slippery to handle with this technique, but do look beautiful once you have mastered the art. The secret of making this rose look full is to twist the centre to form the rose bud before you stitch it in position. Remember the wider the ribbon the larger the rose, the narrower the ribbon the smaller the rose. You will find the petals of this rose look a little more pointed than the folded rose technique.

Folded rose   Concertina rose

Method

Take one metre (1¼yd) of ribbon and fold at an angle of 45 degrees (Fig 1) at the centre.

Fold the ribbon down behind the first fold (Fig 2).

Fold the left-hand ribbon across to the right behind the down ribbon.

Continue folding the ribbon top to bottom, right to left forming a square (Fig 3), always towards the back until all the ribbon is used up (about 20 folds) and keeping your first angle free.

Holding the two ends together in one hand, let go of the folded ribbon allowing it to fall out like a concertina (Fig 4).

Gently pull one of the ribbons to form a rose – it does not matter which ribbon you pull.

Take the centre of the rose and gently twist the ribbon around to form a fuller rose.

With needle and knotted thread go down through the centre of the rose and secure it in place.

If you are making a lot of these roses it is better not to cut of a length of ribbon, but to work from the roll, thereby saving you a lot of surplus small pieces of ribbon. When you pull the ends through, pull the one that is attached to the roll.

Fig 4

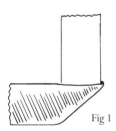
Fig 1

Fig 2

Fig 3

Wire-edged rose

This is the simplest of all the ribbon rose techniques and can be made in a few minutes. It does, however, use a lot of ribbon to make it look full and generous – on average one metre (1¼yd) of 35mm (1⅜") wide ribbon will make a beautiful rose.

Method

Gently manipulate the wire at one end of the ribbon and pull out 10cm (4").

On the opposite end gather up the same wire until it is reduced to about 40cm (½yd).

Fold under one of the gathered ends and twist around twice to form the centre bud (Fig 1), leaving the wire hanging free so that you can hold on to this while forming your rose.

Roll the rest of the gathered ribbon around this centre to form a large soft rose.

Use the wire from the ribbon to twist together to hold the rose in place (Fig 2).

Wire-edged ribbon should not be washed or dry cleaned therefore it is not suitable for fashion or soft furnishing. However, it is ideal for craft items and accessories.

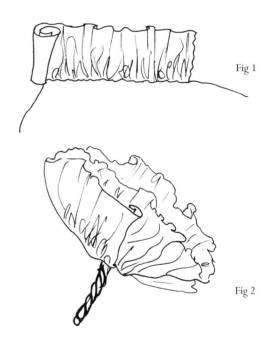

Fig 1

Fig 2

Cabbage rose

Cabbage roses are made in fabric that is cut on the bias grain so they are extremely easy to handle. They can be made large or small using many types of fabric. I chose to make this type of rose to embellish the shoulder line of the wedding dress I designed and made for my daughter-in-law, Amanda. They look beautiful made in silk organza, dupion or crêpe de Chine. You could also make them in soft tweeds or wool using the same fabric as your garment.

Method

Cut one piece of fabric 25cm × 15cm (10" × 6") on the true bias grain.

Fold in half lengthwise.

Make an angle of 45 degrees (Fig 1).

Start to roll from this angle with a slight spiral effect until you have formed a soft cabbage rose. When the roll is completed stitch through all layers at the base to hold the rose in place (Fig 2).

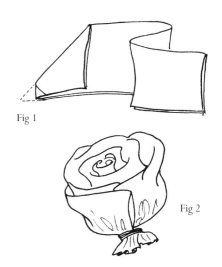

Fig 1

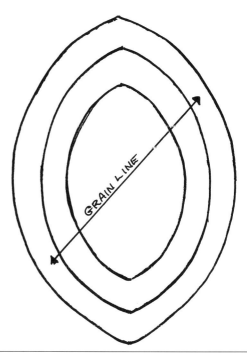

Fig 2

Dior rose

Dior was well known for his fabulous roses and added them to call attention to detail. They cascaded down the backs of evening dresses or at the neckline of tweed suits and, of course, his beautiful hats. You can add a touch of haute couture to embellish your fashion garments too by following his example. The Dior rose is cut in a football shape on the true bias as this gives a lovely soft look and does not get crushed easily as the bias resists wrinkles.

Method

Trace off the pattern in the three sizes and cut your fabric on the true bias.

Fold each petal in half lengthways on the bias grain and make a row of running stitches along the base of the petal 0.5cm (1/4") in from the raw edge.

Gather up the fullness and secure the gathers on each petal.

Start by rolling up the small petal to form a rose-bud and stitch securely to hold in position.

Wrap the medium shape petal around the small bud, add to this the larger petal and stitch them all together.

GRAIN LINE

When all the petals are in place, finish off the base of the rose by simply whip stitching the raw ends together, or by covering all the edges so that the rose can be made detachable and worn on your jacket lapel.

This rose is very versatile and can be made as large as you need depending on your design. More petals can also be added but keep the balance and proportion the same. This rose is so delicate it really is worth the extra effort and looks lovely on millinery with a mixture or textures for the roses.

Ribbon leaves

Ribbon leaves are easy to make and add another dimension to your work. Various widths of ribbon can be used for the leaves up to 5cm (2") wide depending whether you need small or large leaves for your design.

To make the leaves follow the diagrams for one of the four designs illustrated here. Figs 1 to 6 show a gathering thread across the base of the folded ribbon, for a 10mm (⅜") wide ribbon you will need 5cm (2") for Figs 1 to 6, and 8cm (3⅛") for

the 20mm (¾") wide ribbon. Run a gathering thread across the base of the folded ribbon, pull the thread to gather tightly and place on your work, sew the leaf in place and add the roses.

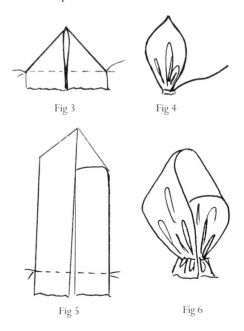

Fig 3   Fig 4

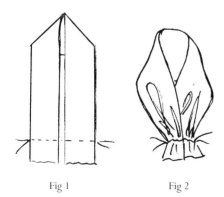

Fig 1   Fig 2   Fig 5   Fig 6

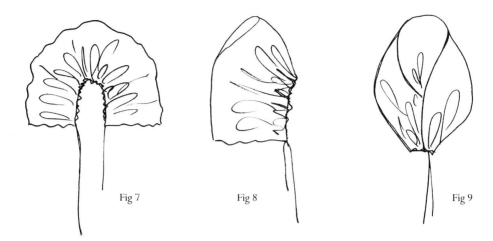

Fig 7   Fig 8   Fig 9

Figs 7, 8 and 9 are for the wire-edged ribbon, which makes a lovely full shaped leaf. You will need roughly 20cm (8") of the 35mm (1¼") wide ribbon. Gather the wire tightly along one edge, fold together and shape into a leaf. The wire-edged ribbon is ideal for making leaves that are added to the stem of a ribbon rose when used for a brooch.

Plaiting and Braiding

It is often difficult to find braids in the colours you need when working on a project. Making your own braid in the colours you need can be fun and easy to do, and it grows very fast. This particular braid can be used on many different projects in both double-faced satin ribbon and using the Russia braid. The fascinating texture of this braid made in two colours, gives the appearance of being made in four different colours, but looks equally good made in one colour to match or contrast with your background.

You will need 4½ times your finished length of each colour in ribbons of the same width. This braid works best using ribbons between 3mm (⅛") and 13mm (½") wide. It can be used for decorating packages, swags or baskets, but it looks wonderful made in the Russia braid and used to trim a Chanel-type jacket.

Two colour braid

Make a loop in one end of both ribbons and place one loop inside the other (Fig 1). Stitch together leaving the second loop free.

Make a loop with the second colour and place through the first loop (Fig 2). Pull down gently on the first loop to fit snugly – this will help to keep the braid neat and even.

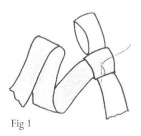
Fig 1

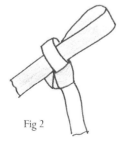
Fig 2

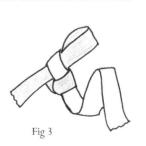
Fig 3

Fig 4

Continue in this way placing one loop inside another (Fig 3) until you have the length you desire.

To finish the plait, simply thread the last ribbon through the loop and machine across the ends. Trim and use as required.

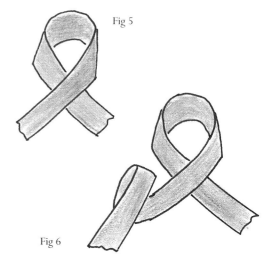

Fig 5

Fig 6

One colour braid

Start in the centre of your ribbon and make the loops following the diagrams in Figs 5 and 6.

The amount of ribbon needed for this one colour braid is the same as for the two colour braid.

Home Furnishings

Opulent cushion

This beautiful ribbon trimmed cushion is very simple to make and requires only the ability to machine in a straight line when placing the ribbons around the central panel of quilting. It complements the envelope cushion and the bolster case lying on the bed quilt (see later projects).

Materials

- Cut two sections of fabric measuring 38cm (15") square, (14" cushion)
- 1 piece of 4oz wadding measuring 19cm (7½")
- 1½ metres (1yd 23") of piping cord
- 1.20cm (1¼yd) of Swiss jacquard
- 1.20cm (1¼yd) of picot-edged petersham
- 1 packet of Bondaweb

Making up

Place your square of wadding in the centre of your fabric (Fig 1) and quilt in 1½cm (½") diagonal squares using a matching thread (Fig 2).

Cut Bondaweb exactly the same width as the jacquard ribbon, and press onto the reverse side of the ribbon. Bond to the petersham ribbon by pressing.

Place the first ribbon 8cm (3") in from the raw edge on the top left-hand side of the cushion pad (Fig 3) and machine stitch along outside edge of the jacquard ribbon only. Position the second ribbon in place under first ribbon up to the stitching line. Stitch again along the outside edge only. Continue to place ribbons in position following the diagram in Fig 3. When all these ribbons are in place, machine the inner edge of jacquard ribbon to complete the design, keeping the ribbons firmly in place. Press over the stitching, being careful to avoid the quilted panel.

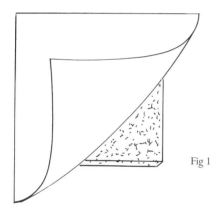

Fig 1

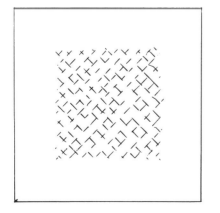

Fig 2

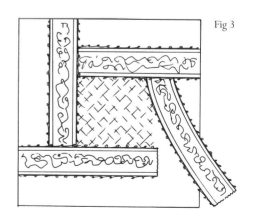

Fig 3

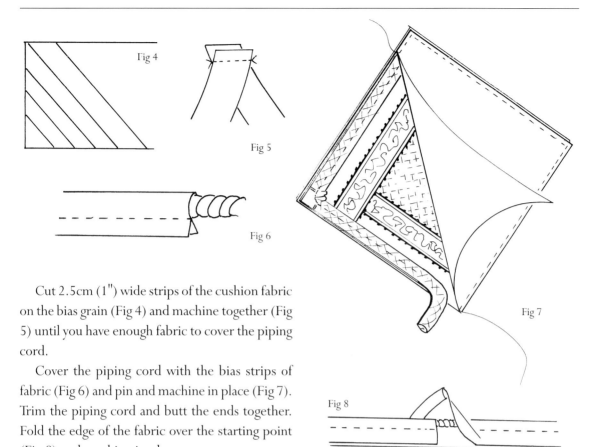

Fig 4

Fig 5

Fig 6

Fig 7

Fig 8

Cut 2.5cm (1") wide strips of the cushion fabric on the bias grain (Fig 4) and machine together (Fig 5) until you have enough fabric to cover the piping cord.

Cover the piping cord with the bias strips of fabric (Fig 6) and pin and machine in place (Fig 7). Trim the piping cord and butt the ends together. Fold the edge of the fabric over the starting point (Fig 8) and machine in place.

Place the back of the cushion over the ribbon work and piping, pin in place. Machine on four sides leaving a 20cm (8") gap on one side of cushion. Turn the cushion to the right side through the gap, making sure the piped corners are neat. Hand stitch the cushion together along open edge, turning in the seam allowance along the back edge.

Bed quilt

This beautiful bed quilt relies for its truly stunning effect on the richness of the lovely Swiss jacquard ribbon combined with the soft picot edge of the petersham ribbon and simplicity of design. Two different ribbons were used to create this rich and interesting texture. The Swiss jacquard ribbon was first bonded onto the picot-edged petersham before being stitched into position, weaving one ribbon under and over the others. This bed quilt was made to fit a 5ft × 7ft bed, but you may wish to alter these measurements to fit your own bed.

Materials

- 5 metres (5½yd) of 130cm (51") wide fabric
- 19 metres (21yd) of picot-edged petersham ribbon, 56mm (2¼") wide
- 19 metres (21yd) of Swiss jacquard 35mm (1⅜") wide
- 5 metres (5½yd) of Vilene 4oz wadding
- 1 packet of Bondaweb (cut into strips the width of jacquard ribbon)
- 1 double size polycotton sheet for backing
- Matching thread to background of jacquard ribbon

Making up

Marking the design

Cut the Bondaweb into strips the width of the jacquard ribbon and press onto the back of the jacquard ribbon. Peel the paper off when cold, and press to bond the jacquard onto the petersham ribbon.

Cut one section of fabric 2½ metres (2yd 27") in length × 130cm (51") – the width of the fabric.

Place the remaining section (also 2½ metres ×

130cm) to one side for use later. This fabric will become your side panels.

To mark the position of the ribbons you will fold and press the fabric to make clear lines:

Take the fabric and fold it across its width 50cm (20") up from the hem (Fig 1) and press a line across. Unfold the fabric.

Fold the fabric in half lengthways and press a line straight down the centre, stopping at the line 50cm (20") from the hem. Leave folded (Fig 2).

Fold the fabric in half again lengthways, placing the folded edge just 1½cm (½") in from the selvedge edge and press again. Leave folded. The folded fabric now measures roughly 2½ metres (2yd 27") by 33cm (13") wide from folded edge to folded edge (Fig 3).

To mark the squares across, fold the fabric about 33cm (13") up from the first line across (which is 50cm/20" from the hem) and press (Fig 4).

Measure up from this line another 33cm (13") and press again. Repeat this process until all the squares are marked, the final crease being approximately 33cm (13") from the top edge (Fig 4).

Open out the fabric and you will now see the design 'creased' into place. Lay the fabric on top of

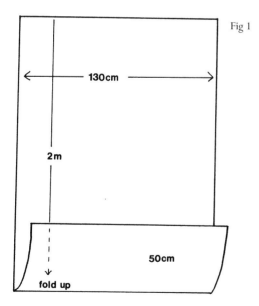

Fig 1

130cm

2m

50cm

fold up

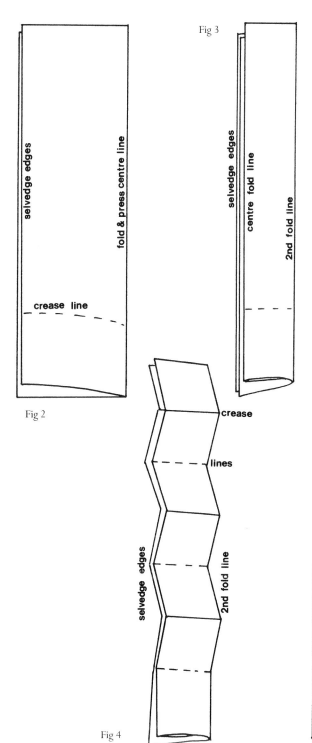

Fig 3

selvedge edges

fold & press centre line

crease line

Fig 2

selvedge edges

centre fold line

2nd fold line

crease

lines

selvedge edges

2nd fold line

Fig 4

the 4oz wadding and pin the two together (Fig 5).

Machine stitch the fabric to the wadding along the crease lines using a long stitch. The design is now clearly marked (Fig 5).

Weaving the ribbon

Cut 3 lengths of ribbon 2 metres (2¼yd) long (the warp ribbons), and 5 lengths of ribbon 130cm (51") long (the width of your centre panel i.e. the weft ribbons).

Centre the warp ribbons over the three vertical lines of stitching. Then, leaving a gap at every other 'crease line' – in order to weave the weft under the warp ribbons at a later stage – carefully machine the warp ribbons in place.

Weave the weft ribbons under and over the warp ribbons, and stitch carefully in place.

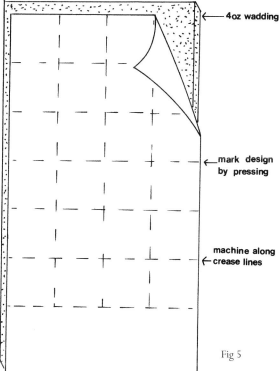

4oz wadding

mark design by pressing

machine along crease lines

Fig 5

Joining the side panels to the centre panel

Using the second section of fabric, fold in half lengthways and trim to measure 2½ metres (2yd 27") × 50cm (20") wide.

Pin and tack the wadding into position on the side panels, using the same method as for the centre panel.

Pin the side panels to the centre panel and machine in place. Open seams by hand, stitching them open and using large stitches to catch the fabric to the wadding. (Do not press as you will flatten the wadding.)

To complete the design, place the ribbon over this seam. Mitre the corners by folding (not cutting) the ribbon (Fig 6). Follow the bottom line of stitching, covering the raw edges of the warp ribbon. Stitch carefully in place (Fig 7).

Place the border ribbon 4cm (1½") from the raw edge of the quilt, mitre the corners to match the centre panel and machine in place (Fig 7).

Fold a 4cm (1½") hem all around the quilt, hand stitch in position with a large herringbone stitch onto the wadding to hold the hem in place.

Line the quilt with a matching polycotton sheet, which is lighter and easier to handle than traditional curtain lining and gives a nicer feeling of comfort to the quilt.

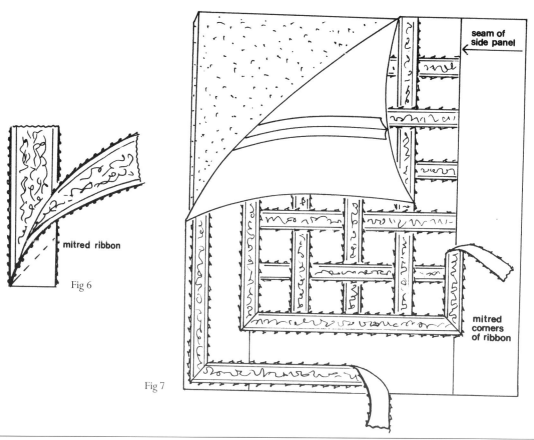

mitred ribbon

Fig 6

seam of side panel

mitred corners of ribbon

Fig 7

Bolster case

The bolster size used on this bed was 1.5 metres (5ft) in length, measured 24cm (9½") in diameter 75cm (29½") in circumference and was made from feathers.

Materials

- 75cm × 130cm (29½" × 51") of fabric for centre panel
- 2 × 75cm × 15cm (29½" × 5⅞") for the side panels
- 2 × 75cm × 15cm (29½" × 5⅞") strips of fabric for buttoned ends
- 8 metres (8yd 28") of picot-edged petersham ribbon, 56mm (2¼") wide
- 8 metres (8yd 28") of Swiss jacquard ribbon 35mm (1⅜") wide
- 1 packet of Bondaweb (cut into strips the width of the jacquard ribbon)
- 2 zips measuring 54cm (21") long for the opening
- 1.5 metres (1¼yd) of piping cord
- 2 tassels (optional)

Making up: order of work

Join the side panels to the centre panel and press the seams open (the panel now measures 75cm × 160cm/29½" × 63" wide). Mark the centre point of the panel.

Cut two lengths of ribbon 75cm (29½") in length (the petersham and the Swiss jacquard) and keep to one side (these ribbons will cover the panel's seams).

To form the diagonal pattern, place ribbons around the centre point in diagonal squares of roughly 27cm (10½") weaving them under and over each other, as for Fig 1, in the same manner

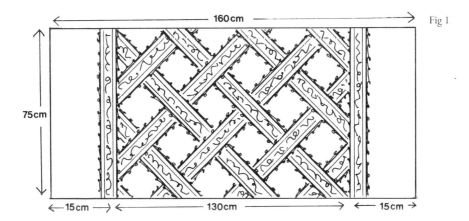

Fig 1

160cm

75cm

15cm 130cm 15cm

as the bed quilt. Machine in place and press well.

Place the two 75cm (29½") lengths of ribbon at either side of the panel to cover the seams and the ends of the ribbons. Stitch in place and press. Do stop and check that these last two ribbons run parallel to the ribbons on the quilt before stitching them in place (Fig 2).

Fold the bolster case in half lengthways and machine together the last 24cm (9½") at each end. Press the seam open.

Place the zips, with the openings facing each other, at the centre of the bolster. Pin and tack in position. Hand stitch in place (Fig 2).

Cut a length of fabric on the bias grain 4cm (1½") wide and long enough to cover the piping cord. Fold the fabric over the piping cord and machine in place close to the cord using the zipper foot of the sewing machine. When this is complete, cut the covered piping in half and stitch one length to each end of the bolster case 1cm (⅜") in from the edge.

Take the 15cm (5⅞") wide strips of fabric and join the ends to form a circle using a 1cm (⅜") seam allowance.

Place these two circles of fabric over the piping cord at each end of the bolster case and pin in place. Using the previous row of stitching as a guide, stitch these circle strips in place (Fig 3).

Pleat the fabric into the centre to form a neat circle and place a large covered button over the centre point, or finish off with a large fat tassel (Fig 4).

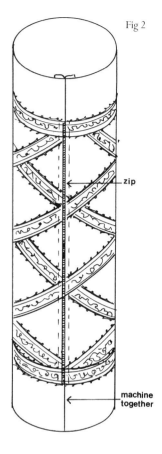

Fig 2

zip

machine together

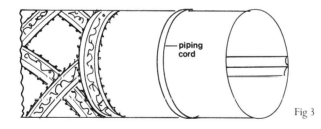

piping cord

Fig 3

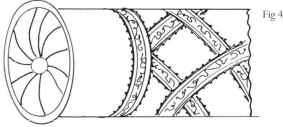

Fig 4

Envelope cushion

This unusual cushion is simplicity itself and a wonderful idea for a beginner to try. The simple square shape has been given a variety of treatments. The fabric was first quilted on each of the four corners over a 4oz wadding, then a wide band of picot-edged petersham ribbon was bonded to the Swiss jacquard ribbon and top stitched around the edge of the square. The ribbon was folded to form a mitre on each corner of the square, rather than cutting and stitching. A cross of velcro was made and used for the closure of this cushion. Finally, to hide the fastening and complete the design, a rosette was made from the beautiful jacquard ribbon by pleating this into a circle. The inner pad for this particular cushion was made from the same fabric as the outer shell, but equally a contrasting fabric could be used depending on your colour scheme. You could pick up other colours in your cushions to co-ordinate your furnishing scheme. To fit the measurements shown below, a 36cm (14") cushion was made for the inner pad.

Materials

- Two pieces of fabric measuring 50cm (20") square (allowance for 1½cm/½" seam)
- 2 metres (2¼yd) of picot-edged petersham, 56mm (2¼") wide
- 2 metres (2¼yd) of Swiss jacquard, 35mm (1⅜") wide
- 30cm (12") of Swiss jacquard for the rosette
- 16cm (6½") of velcro for fastening
- One piece of 4oz wadding, 33cm (13") square (cut into four sections diagonally)
- Packet of Bondaweb cut into strips the same width as the jacquard ribbon

Making up

Cut wadding into four sections diagonally. With the wrong side of the fabric facing you, place the triangles of wadding in each corner 6½cm (2½") in from the raw edge. Pin and tack in position and quilt over the wadding in diagonal rows, with the right side of the fabric facing you (Fig 1).

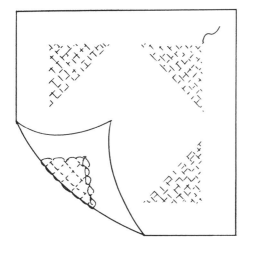

Fig 1

Place the second piece of fabric over the quilted section, right sides together, and pin and machine together on all sides with a 1½cm (½") seam allowance, leaving a 20cm (8") gap on one side to turn cushion cover through. Trim the corners, turn through and press carefully. Hand stitch the open edges together (Fig 2).

Cut the Bondaweb into strips the exact width of the jacquard ribbon, and bond to the ribbon by placing the adhesive side (rough side) to the ribbon and pressing with a very warm iron. Peel off the paper when it is quite cold (and not before). Place the jacquard ribbon centrally along the petersham ribbon and bond the two ribbons together by pressing them carefully in position (Fig 3).

Pin the bonded ribbons in place around the edge of cushion square (Fig 4) and machine carefully on the edge of the jacquard ribbon, on the outer edge first. Fold the ribbon carefully on each corner as you stitch, to form a mitre. Stitch a second row carefully around the inner edges. Fold the end of the ribbon at right angles to form the last mitre (Fig 4). (Press machining on ribbon being

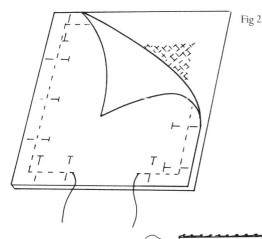

Fig 2

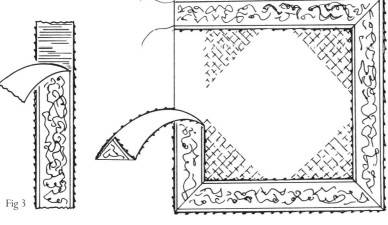

Fig 3

Fig 4

Fig 5

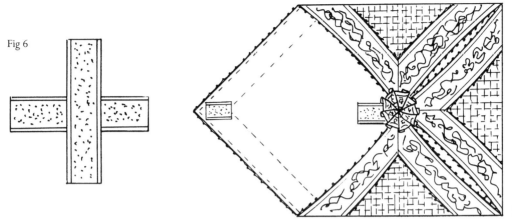

Fig 6

Fig 7

very careful to avoid the quilted section.)

Pleat the 30cm (12") piece of jacquard ribbon (Fig 5) to form a rosette, and stitch pleats together on one edge only allow rosette to form a circle. Stitch the rosette to the very edge of one corner of the cushion square.

Separate the velcro, cut the rough section in half and stitch to form a cross (Fig 6). Cut the remaining smooth section of velcro into four pieces and stitch in place by hand on each corner of the cushion pad on the wrong side.

Place the velcro square in the centre of the cushion pad and wrap the cushion square around the pad (Fig 7).

Tartan-trimmed table mats

Tartan is a favourite of designers the world over for its timeless classic appearance, and these lovely (reversible) table mats trimmed with tartan ribbon, make a delightfully simple introduction to embellishing your home furnishings with ribbon. As usual, it is always the careful finishing touches that make your room look complete and give it that cared-for co-ordinated look. The table mats are quite simple to make and only require the ability to machine in a straight line.

To make your table warm and inviting or festive for Christmas time, a furnishing fabric in dark red cotton jacquard was used for one side of the mat, with the reverse side being made in bottle green viyella. In the centre of the mat a 4oz. Vilene wadding was used. The ribbon trimming was made up by using two widths of different tartan ribbons – the wider ribbon is the Cameron tartan and the narrower ribbon on the reverse side of the mat is the Royal Stewart tartan, which makes a striking contrast to the bottle green fabric. To keep a nice crisp edge around the table mats, the ribbons were stitched together along one edge, and then placed over the three layers of the table mats.

Tips for easy sewing

Although the same width ribbon could be used on both sides of the table mats, you will find it much easier to handle this trimming if a narrower width of ribbon is used on the reverse side, then by hand stitching the narrower ribbon in place over your machining, you will be able to cover the machine stitches and keep the ribbon nice and straight.

Materials

🎀 70cm (27½") of 90cm (1yd) wide furnishing cotton will make 4 mats (35cm/13¾" for two)

🎀 70cm (27½") of 90cm (1yd) wide fabric for backing

🎀 50cm (20") of 150cm (5ft) wide – 4oz Vilene wadding

🎀 1.70cm (1yd 31") of 78mm (3") wide Cameron tartan ribbon for one place mat

🎀 2.85cm (3yd 4") of 38mm (1½") wide Royal Stewart tartan ribbon for one place mat

🎀 Matching thread for stitching

Making up

The fabric and ribbon should be washed and pressed before you begin to cut out or sew to reduce the risk of shrinkage (as table mats are washed frequently).

Cut fabrics and Vilene wadding into pieces measuring 36cm × 46cm (14" × 18"). Pin all three layers together and tack in place. This tacking is very important (Fig 1).

Stitch together 1.70cm (1yd 31") of Cameron and Royal Stewart tartan ribbons together along the very edge. Press stitching and ribbon carefully (Fig 2).

Open the ribbon out and place over the raw edges of the table mat. Pin in position, the wider ribbon on the red side and the narrower ribbon onto the bottle green side. Pin carefully as you work, keeping the ribbon smooth and straight on both sides. Make a mitre in each of the four corners, on both sides, by folding the fabric at an angle (Fig 3). Machine stitch the wider ribbon in place (Fig 4).

Turn mat to reverse side and hand stitch the narrower ribbon in place with neat slip stitches (Fig 5). Do not press as you will flatten the wadding.

Still on reverse side, place the second narrow ribbon over the machine stitching (which was made when stitching wide ribbon in place) and mitre the corners by folding as you did before. Slip stitch in place (Fig 5).

If you wish to use the same width ribbon on both sides of your table mats, it is very important that when the ribbons are pinned in place, they are also tacked in position before you begin to machine, otherwise you will not be able to keep

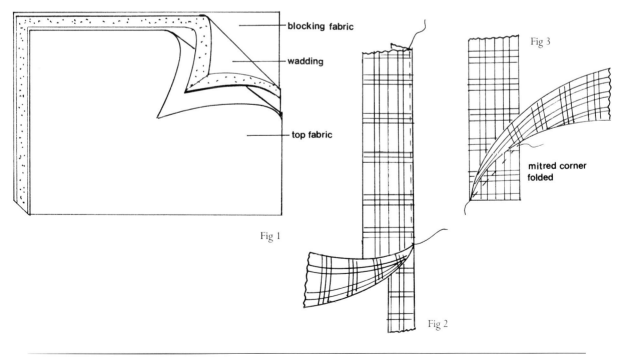

blocking fabric

wadding

top fabric

Fig 1

Fig 3

mitred corner folded

Fig 2

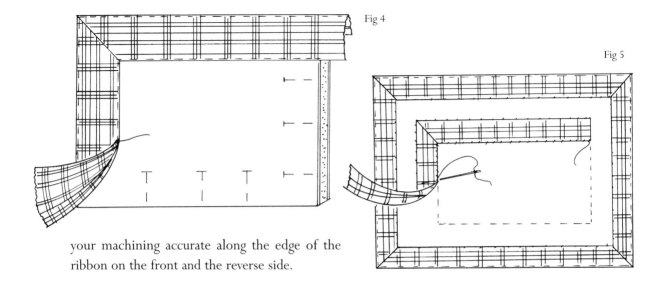

Fig 4

Fig 5

your machining accurate along the edge of the ribbon on the front and the reverse side.

Matching napkins

Bottle green viyella fabric was used for the napkins to match the reversible table mats. Each napkin measures 45cm (17¾") square and uses 2 metres (2¼yd) of the polyester Cameron tartan ribbon 75mm (3") wide. Before you start to sew, wash the fabric and ribbon to eliminate any shrinkage as these napkins will be washed frequently.

Fold and press the tartan ribbon in half lengthways, making sure that the front side is slightly narrower than the back – this will ensure that the back edge of the ribbon is machined in place.

Place the folded edge of the ribbon over the edge of the napkin, pin in place, making sure the wider side of the ribbon is placed at the back.

Make a folded mitre on each corner of the napkin, the same as the table mats, machine in place. Press carefully.

For the Christmas table, the green napkins were tied with a bow in red satin ribbon and decorated with a gold organza rose.

Picture bows and rosettes

Rosettes

Add a lovely splash of colour to your rooms with picture bows and rosettes – they are guaranteed to give you an uplift and give your surroundings a brand new look. For added texture, two ribbons were bonded together for this rosette, using the picot-edged petersham ribbon and the polyester Buchanan tartan ribbon, but if you wish just use one ribbon. The rosette gives a tailored, more formal look to your pictures as opposed to the bow which has a much softer feel.

Materials

- 1 metre 50cm of 56mm (1yd 23½") wide picot-edged petersham ribbon in red
- 1 metre 50cm (1yd 23½") of 38mm (1½") wide polyester Buchanan tartan
- 35cm (13¾") of gold satin ribbon, 22mm (¾") wide
- Bondaweb, one packet
- Fabric glue

Method

For the rosette, cut 60cm (2¾") off both lengths of ribbon. Cut the Bondaweb the same width as the tartan ribbon and press onto the back of this ribbon following the manufacturer's instructions.

For the tail section, centre the tartan ribbon onto the petersham ribbon (Fig 1). For the rosette, place the tartan ribbon close to one edge of the petersham and bond the two ribbons together.

Mark the folds of the pleats at 3cm (1¼") intervals. Pleat the ribbon, pressing it with your finger, making sure the inner edge is overlapping to form a circle as you pleat (Fig 2). Pin to hold in place.

Hand stitch the pleats in position using a double-waxed thread for extra strength. Place the end of the ribbon under the first pleat and sew together.

Make a satin rose and place in the centre of the rosette, following the directions for the folded rose in the rose making chapter.

Make a point at one end of the tail section and glue in place (Fig 4).

Hand stitch the tail section firmly in place behind the centre of the rosette (Fig 3).

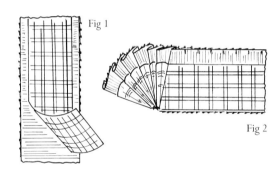

Fig 1

Fig 2

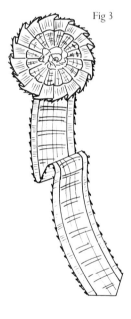

Fig 3

Fig 4

Picture bows

A variety of wide ribbons can be used for picture bows. You will find that the petersham ribbon will give stability and elegance to all your pictures. The one I have used here is the picot-edged petersham, with a polyester gingham ribbon added for extra texture, but the plain petersham ribbon used on its own looks equally good.

Materials for the double bow

- 🎀 1 metre 80cm (2yd) of 56mm (2¼") wide picot-edged petersham ribbon
- 🎀 1 metre 70cm (1yd 31") of 38mm (1½") wide polyester gingham
- 🎀 Bondaweb
- 🎀 Fabric glue

Method

Cut two lengths of the petersham ribbon, 40cm (16").

Cut two lengths of the gingham ribbon, 36cm (14").

Fold each of the four ribbon sections with a small overlap at the centre back and glue in place (Fig 1).

Pleat one petersham and one gingham bow, tie them together with narrow ribbon or florist's tape (Fig 2).

Repeat for the second bows and tie all four bows together (Fig 3), opening out the bows and arranging them to look pretty.

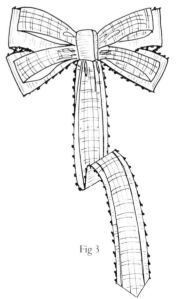

Fig 1

Fig 2

Fig 3

Bond the two remaining lengths of ribbons together. Fold to a point at one end and glue in place. Pleat the top end of the tail to reduce the width to a third and fold it tightly over the centre of the double bow. Hand stitch or glue in position (Fig 3).

This bow can be made single and without a second ribbon bonded on to it (Fig 4).

Maltese Cross rosette

This can be made with the same ribbon and dimensions as the bow, but instead of gluing the bow together as in Fig 1 for the bow, it is better to machine it together.

Fold the loops lengthways and overlap by 1cm (½"), machine flat together (as in Fig 1 for the bow).

With the seam in the centre back, tie each loop tightly around the centre with narrow ribbon.

Place the loops across each other (Fig 5) and tie tightly together.

Make a large covered button with fabric and sew in the centre to hide the ribbon ties (Fig 6).

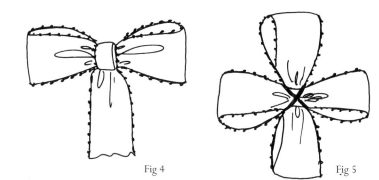

Fig 4

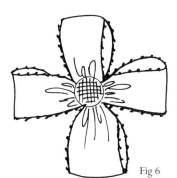

Fig 5

Fig 6

Roman blind

For elegantly tailored windows Roman blinds are the perfect choice. They look their best made from a non-stiffened good quality fabric with an even weave. You will need enough fabric to cover your windows plus seam allowances. The blind that is illustrated here is decorated with two ribbons bonded together – one is a beautiful woven jacquard ribbon with the picot-edged petersham ribbon. After bonding the ribbons together they are then stitched in place, hiding the stitching from the tapes and rings attached to the back of the blind.

You will need enough ribbon to cover the length of the blind three times plus the width for the top and bottom of the blind.

Materials

- Enough fabric and lining to cover the window plus 2.5cm (1") for side turnings and 15cm (6") for top and bottom hems
- Picot-edged petersham ribbon, 56mm (2¼") wide × 3 times the length and twice the width of the blind
- Jacquard ribbon 35mm (1⅜") wide × 3 times the length and twice the width
- Bondaweb to bond the two ribbons together
- Tape and rings for the back of the blind, three times the length
- Matching thread to ribbon

Making up

Cut out the fabric and lining to the same size and place right sides together, machine side seams and lower hem 12mm (½"). Turn to the right sides and press. Turn up hem 6cm (2½"). Press in place but leave free. Do the same at the top edge.

Lay the blind flat, lining uppermost, and position the tapes vertically on each side 12mm (½")

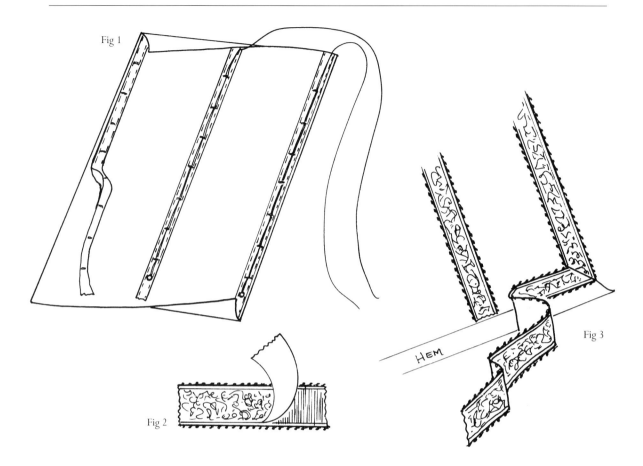

Fig 1

Fig 2

Fig 3

HEM

in from the edge and place one tape down the centre (the raw edges of the tape will tuck in to the hem). Machine close to the edges of the tape through all thicknesses (Fig 1).

Cut the Bondaweb to fit exactly the jacquard ribbon and following the instructions on the packet, bond the jacquard ribbon to the picot-edged petersham ribbon (Fig 2).

With the right side of the blind facing you, place one strip of bonded ribbon vertically down the centre, covering the machine stitching for the tape. Cut off at hem level (Fig 3).

Place the second ribbon strip down the right-hand side of the blind, folding the ribbon into a neat mitred corner at the hem. Place the ribbon along the hem line over the centre ribbon (Fig 3), continue along the left-hand side of the blind, folding the ribbon into a mitred corner again. Machine in place just inside the edge of the jacquard ribbon.

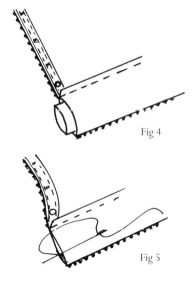

Fig 4

Fig 5

Continue to place the ribbon across the top edge of the blind folding into a mitre around the corner with a half fold on the last corner to make it look neat.

Hand stitch hems in place, leave sides open for baton and slip in (Fig 4).

Hand sew sides of hem together (Fig 5). Fit the blind in the usual way.

Curtain trims

Those special touches carefully made to co-ordinate with your cushions, lampshades or rugs make your home look especially cherished. One simple way of doing this is by adding a splash of colour to your voile curtains for any of the rooms in your house. For the kitchen curtains I chose the Buchanan tartan, but the gingham ribbons would look lovely too. For the living room I have used the wide satin ribbons in three colourways plus the petersham ribbon across the hem. For added colour and texture the curtain pole was also covered in red satin ribbon for both curtains.

Buchanan tartan kitchen curtains

Materials

- Tartan trim in two widths. Buchanan tartan 38mm (1½") wide and 75mm (3") wide.
- You will need enough of the 38mm (1½") wide ribbon to cover the width of your curtain plus the hanging loops for the top edge. Each loop measures 26cm (10") folded in half to 13cm (5")
- 75mm (3") wide ribbon, twice the length of the curtain, folded in half lengthways.
- Heading tape

Making up

Fold down the top edge of the curtain by 5cm (2") and press. Fold the 75mm (3") wide ribbon in half lengthways and press. Make sure that one side is fractionally wider than the other. Place this ribbon down the sides of the voile with the wider side at the back and sew in place (Fig 1).

Place the heading tape at the back of the curtain starting from the edge of the tartan ribbon and covering the raw edge of the voile and machine in place.

With the right side of the voile facing you, place the 38mm (1½") wide ribbon over the machining for the heading tape. Machine ribbon along the lower edge only.

Cut the remaining 38mm (1½") wide ribbon into 26cm (10") long strips for the loops, fold in half and pin them at 19cm (7½") intervals apart, making sure they fit against the lower edge of the ribbon (Fig 2).

Machine along the top edge of the ribbon catching the loops in place.

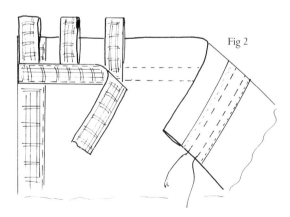

Fig 1

Fig 2

Optional extra

The curtain pole was covered with red satin ribbon with small pieces of red felt at each end. A double-faced satin, 22mm (¾") wide was used (Fig 3).

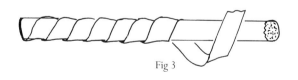

Fig 3

Satin stripe trim – voile curtain

Materials

- 50mm (2") wide red double-faced satin ribbon, the width of your curtain for the top edge plus the two sides.
- 38mm (1⅜") wide red double-faced satin ribbon for the hanging loops. Each loop is cut 20cm (8") long and set 14cm (5½") apart
- 22mm (¾") wide double-faced satin in red, yellow and green
- 56mm (2¼") wide picot-edged petersham the width of your curtains for the hem
- Bondaweb, one packet
- Pencil pleat heading

Method

Make a 2.5cm (1") hem down both sides of each curtain and press.

Cut the Bondaweb to fit the width of the 50mm (2") wide ribbon and press onto the back of it. Place this bonded ribbon onto both sides of each curtain along the edge, press carefully in position then machine in place close to the edge of the ribbon. Reserve the rest of this ribbon for the top edge.

Press the Bondaweb onto the back of the 22mm (¾") wide ribbon and place them in sequence red, yellow, green, red, yellow, green, down the length of the curtain roughly 16cm (6½") apart. Press each ribbon in position and then machine in place.

·With the wrong side of the heading tape facing the right side of the curtain, overlapping by 1cm (½") machine the tape in place (Fig 1). Fold over to the wrong side of the curtain and machine the lower edge in place. Fold the ends under and hand stitch the edge of the tape (Fig 2).

Cut the 38mm (1⅜") wide ribbon into 20cm (8") lengths and pin them 14cm (5½") apart. Using the reserve of the 50mm (2") wide ribbon, place across the top edge of the curtain over the pinned loops and press carefully in place, removing the pins as you press. Machine in place. Hand stitch the edges together.

Turn a 2.5cm (1") hem onto the right side of the curtain and press in place. Cut the Bondaweb to fit the width of the petersham ribbon and position this over the hem along the edge of the curtain. Machine in place (Fig 3).

The picot-edged petersham ribbon cannot be washed but will dry clean well. If this curtain will need frequent washing it is better to use the satin ribbon on the hem as well as this washes and irons well.

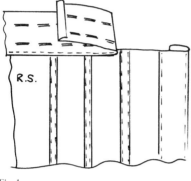

Fig 1

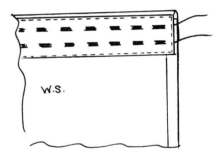

Fig 2

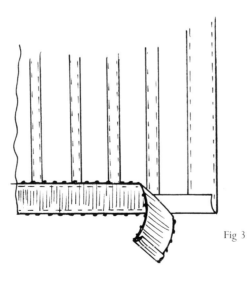

Fig 3

Fashion

Ladies/gentlemen's waistcoat

Waistcoats are wonderful garments to wear and such a versatile addition to your wardrobe. Short or long, fitted or straight, with or without collars – they can be used for any occasion. Throughout the history of fashion, waistcoats have always remained popular, either for warmth or as a flamboyant adornment to an otherwise plain garment. Part of their popularity is the comparative ease of making a waistcoat, as opposed to a dress or jacket for instance, where sleeves must be fitted with accuracy and care. The making up instructions given here can be used with any commercial pattern you buy, with or without the ribbon panels. These instructions are not readily available on the market today, but the techniques I have shared with you are a manufacturing method used for accuracy and speed that you will find easy to follow (they are not the couture method).

The beautiful waistcoat featured here is really luxurious to wear. Woven in the richly textured Swiss jacquard ribbon and using the simple plain weave design, makes it easy for you to personalise your own waistcoats. The illustrations show how to adapt any commercial pattern of your choice. The woven front panel has been shaped to make it more economical, but equally you could weave the whole front panel if you wish.

Pattern adaptation for waistcoat panel

To separate the front panel mark a line 17cm (6¾") in from the front edge and draw a line parallel to this front edge, up to the beginning of the front neck line (Fig 1). Mark a point 14cm (5½") down from the shoulder line and draw a gently curving line from this point to meet the straight line. Cut along this line to separate the panels and add the seam allowances back to these two panels (Figs 1 and 2). Mark your grain line.

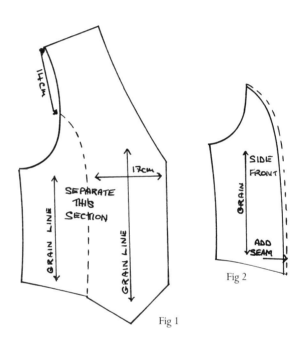

Fig 1

Fig 2

Materials — ribbon panel

- 50cm (20") of Vilene Ultrasoft iron-on interfacing
- 20 metres (20yd) Jacquard ribbon, 20mm (¾") wide
- Glass-headed pins
- 1 cork board covered in polycotton for the ribbon weaving (I used a 40cm × 61cm (16" × 24") bath mat)

- 80cm (32") of 112cm (44") wide fabric for back panels and side front panel
- 1 metre (1yd) of lining
- 6 small buttons
- Small buckle for back belt fastening

Method

Warp ribbons

Taking the separated front panel, cut a section of interfacing slightly larger than your front panel (Fig 3).

Place your interfacing onto the covered cork board adhesive side up.

Mark your grain lines on the interfacing straight down the centre of the panel and across the panel as shown in Figs 1 and 3.

Pin the first ribbon straight down your grain line, pin at top and bottom, making sure the ribbon is firmly anchored (Fig 4). Pin out the rest of the warp ribbons in the same way, side by side, edges touching, working either side of your grain line until the interfacing is covered.

Weft ribbons

Weave your first weft ribbon along your centre grain line, weaving under one, over one, under one to the end of the row.

Pin ribbon firmly in place (Fig 4).

Continue weaving either side of this grain-line ribbon until your panel is finished, following the instructions for the plain weave.

When the weaving is complete place a dry cloth over the weaving and press with a steam iron. Remove the pins, press again on the reverse side with a damp cloth and your panel is now ready to make up.

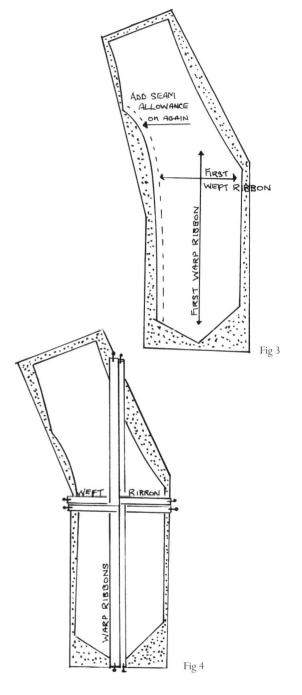

Fig 3

Fig 4

Making up the waistcoat

Place your pattern onto the woven ribbons, matching up your grain line and cut it out.

Machine stitch all around the edge of your cut-out section 1cm (⅜") in from the edge (Fig 5).

To strengthen and stabilise the front edges of your waistcoat, turn the panel to the wrong side and place a stay tape or 3mm (⅛") wide ribbon 1cm (⅜") in from the raw edges as shown in Fig 6 and machine in position. This will keep your woven panel permanently in good shape.

Pin and machine the side front panels to the woven sections, press seams towards the side seam (Fig 7).

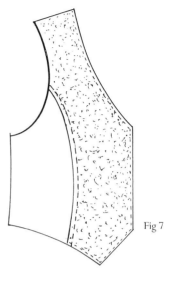

Fig 7

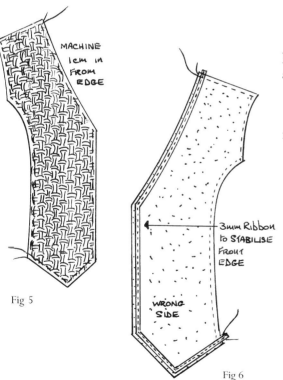

MACHINE 1cm in FROM EDGE

Fig 5

3mm Ribbon to STABILISE FRONT EDGE

WRONG SIDE

Fig 6

With right sides together, place lining over front panels, pin in position and machine together around armhole, front edge and lower edge.

Leave shoulder and side seams open (Fig 8).

Trim seams, clip curves and turn through to right side. Press carefully.

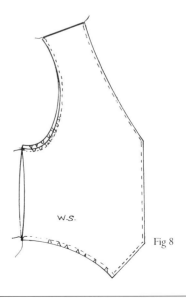

W.S.

Fig 8

With the right sides together, place the lining over the back panel, pin in place and machine around armhole edges only. Trim seams, clip curves. Press. **Do not turn through to the right side** (Fig 9).

Cut two belt sections approximately 7cm × 30cm (2¾4" × 11¾"), fold in half lengthways and stitch on two sides (Fig 10). Trim and turn to right side, press pin in place on back panel into side seams.

Place the front waistcoat panels between the two layers of the back panel.

Feed the side seams and front shoulder seams carefully in place (Fig 11).

Machine through all layers at side seams, shoulder and around back neck edge, being sure to keep stitching accurate around neck and shoulder edges. Trim seams, clip curves, press stitching.

Machine across lower back edge leaving a gap in the centre to pull the waistcoat panel through. **Fold up the front panel points** to avoid catching them in the seam.

Pull front panels through lower back opening. Baste all edges around waistcoat and press carefully. Remove all tacking stitches and press again. Hand stitch lower edges together. Make buttonholes, add buttons. Sew back buckles in place.

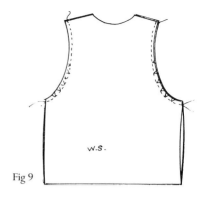

Fig 9

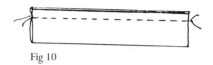

Fig 10

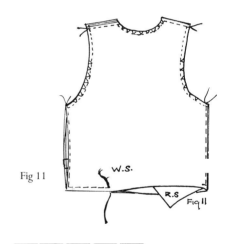

Fig 11

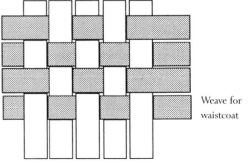

Weave for waistcoat

Silk painted waistcoat

This beautiful pure silk waistcoat woven with gold lamé ribbon uses the fabric and ribbon weaving technique. I designed and made this waistcoat to demonstrate the variation in a simple weave. To achieve this you will need to cut the fabric into 5cm (2") wide strips and work in the plain weave with the 7mm (¼") wide gold lamé ribbon in the warp and weft, forming a vertical stripe. However, the side panels have the gold ribbon in the weft only, making them look completely different and forming a horizontal stripe. The lovely rich jewel colours of the fabric were hand painted by Mary Day.

Long shaped waistcoat

This flattering long shaped waistcoat with deep front and split centre back, fabric and ribbon woven lapels, is made in ivory silk taffeta. The fabric is cut on the bias, 3cm (1¼") wide, stitched, turned and pressed. Plain weave is used for the lapels and the bias weave for the back panel with the 7mm (¼") gold lamé ribbon. Gold braid was stitched along the front side seams and the edges of the back panel. Corded piping was used as a finish for the neckline.

Ladies detachable collar

A detachable collar is a wonderfully easy way to totally change the look of a simple dress or jacket – any number of colour combinations can be used to achieve the look you need. The colours chosen here to wear on a tan silk dress were the softer shades influenced by a trip to Egypt. Two shades of turquoise, cream, beige and black were used in the warp ribbons, with just the cream ribbon woven across the weft. Stronger colours would look stunning on a black or navy dress, or try velvet ribbons woven with gold ribbon onto a velvet jacket for a truly rich texture with a feel of luxury.

The pattern given here will fit onto a double-breasted dress that buttons 5cm (2") above the waistline.

Materials

- 7 metres (7¾yd) double-faced satin ribbon, 3mm (⅛") wide in black
- 7 metres (7¾yd) single- or double-faced satin ribbon, 7mm (¼") wide in dark turquoise
- 7 metres (7¾yd) single- or double-faced satin ribbon, 7mm (¼") wide in pale turquoise
- 7 metres (7¾yd) single- or double-faced satin ribbon, 7mm (¼") wide in beige
- 15 metres (16½yd) single- or double-faced satin ribbon, 7mm wide (¼") in cream
- 30cm (12") of Vilene Ultrasoft iron-on interfacing
- 30cm (12") of lining fabric, plus fabric to make a bias-covered edging on neckline
- Marker pen

Method

For two squares = 2.5cm (1")

Add a 1cm (⅜") seam allowance onto the centre back and the outer edge of the collar only. Cut out the pattern (Fig 1).

Cut out the interfacing slightly larger than the collar pattern, draw the collar shape onto the interfacing marking the grain lines (Fig 2).

Using the narrow black ribbon, place the first warp ribbon along the grain line and pin in place (Fig 2).

Working to the right of this line, pin the following ribbons in sequence, dark turquoise, pale turquoise, cream, beige and black. Repeat this sequence until the warp is complete, reversing the order when you work to the left of the first ribbon.

Weave the weft ribbons with the cream ribbon only starting at the grain line. Follow the instructions for the plain weave to complete the weaving.

Place the pattern onto the finished weaving, cut out the collar and machine around the edge just inside your seam allowance. Press.

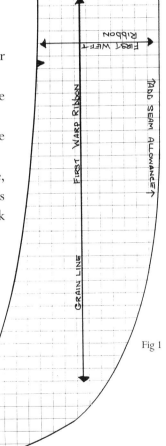

ADD SEAM

←5"→ ←12.5cm→

Ribbon

FIRST WEFT

FIRST WARP Ribbon

ADD SEAM ALLOWANCE →

GRAIN LINE

Fig 1

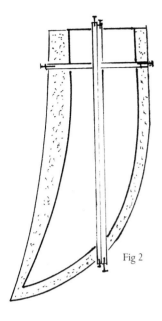

Fig 2

Fig 3

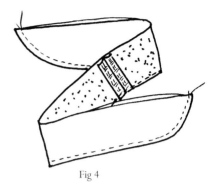

Fig 4

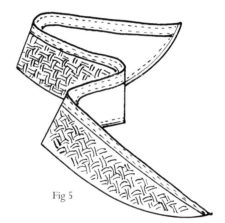

Fig 5

With right sides together machine the centre back seam of collar and lining. Press open (Fig 3).

Stitch collar sections together leaving neck edge open, trim seams, turn and press, under stitch all around edge of lining (Fig 4).

Machine the neck edge of the collar flat together.

Finish the raw edges along the neckline with a folded bias trimming (Fig 4).

The collar can then either be sewn in place, or for speedy changes, small press studs attached to the neckline and to the collar would make it very adaptable.

Appliqué on ladies' jacket

The motif on the back of this navy jacket is taken from a family crest and interpreted in ribbon weaving – the jewel colours were inspired by the Versace collection. Eight colours were used in the warp ribbons and eight colours in the weft ribbons using the simple plain weave. The secret of making this particular appliqué look part of the jacket is the placing of the 3mm (⅛") wide ribbon between each coloured ribbon in both the warp and weft ribbons, because this ribbon matches exactly the colour of the jacket. The crossed logs on the lower part of the design is made by using two shades of tan ribbon, 10mm (⅜") wide but without the narrow ribbon.

Weave a large square of plain weave in your chosen colours, placing one narrow ribbon that matches your background fabric between each coloured warp and weft ribbon. Finish as far as the pressing stage, but do not trim it yet.

Draw your chosen design onto a sheet of Bondaweb and press onto the back of the ribbon weaving. Cut around the shape you drew on the Bondaweb through the ribbons, peel off the backing paper, place the ribbon shape onto the back of your jacket (take care to check the position), place a dry cloth over the woven piece and press in place.

Machine the woven crest in place with a close satin stitch using a matching thread to the jacket. Press carefully.

Add the gold braid by hand around the edge of the appliqué.

The lower part of the design is handled in the same way. First of all stabilise a piece of navy fabric by pressing Vilene Ultrasoft iron-on interfacing onto the back of it.

Secondly, after weaving a section of tan ribbons, press Bondaweb onto the back of the weaving. Draw the log shapes (or your chosen design) onto the Bondaweb and cut out. Peel away the backing and press the two logs into position onto the right side of the navy fabric. The logs are then machined into position using a close satin stitch and a navy thread to match the jacket fabric.

Thirdly, the shape of the small crest is drawn onto the Bondaweb and pressed onto the back of the navy fabric. The shape is then cut out and placed in position at the lower part of the coloured crest, over the coloured weaving and pressed carefully into place.

This is then machined in place with a close satin stitch using a matching thread.

Amanda's Wedding Gown

Wedding dress panels

The Wedding Dress, the magic, the mystery and, of course, the dream – every young girl has one. That moment of sheer delight when you see the bride in her wedding dress before the congregation. Lucky too, is the bride who has a couture gown, hand sewn, made to measure, designed to enhance the true beauty of her body. The decision to make your wedding dress provides you with a unique opportunity that is rare in the world today – to have something completely original and to indulge in beautiful fabrics and trimmings to a high standard of workmanship and design.

Amanda's wedding gown

The wedding gown I designed and made for my daughter-in-law, Amanda, was made entirely of pure silk, consisting of three layers of fabric. The outer layer is pure silk dupion lined with silk habotai, and interlined with pure silk organza. It is this unseen, but crucial, layer of pure silk organza which gives the gown its body and richness that all haute couture garments possess. The design of the gown is very classic: it has a princess line seaming on the front and back bodice. The waistline was lowered 5cm (2") and curved slightly around the back. Soft pleats fall from the side front and side back panels to give a smoother slimmer look than traditional gathers. Nottingham lace was inserted into the back panels, front bodice, cuff edges, neckline and hemline. The stunningly attractive front panel and deep cuffs were woven into the bias weave with the fabric and ribbon technique, but using the trimming and tape maker method. You can adapt a commercial pattern of your choice to make a panel similar to the one on Amanda's dress. Weave the front panel and cuffs after all fitting adjustments have been made to your dress pattern.

Materials

- The fabric and ribbon weaving for the front of Amanda's gown was made with the aid of the trimming and tape maker, using the 12mm (½") width. You will need an extra 1 metre (1¼yd) of your dress fabric for the weaving.
- 15 metres (18¾yd) double-faced satin, 3mm (⅛") wide to match your dress (wedding white)
- Glass-headed pins
- Covered cork board (I used a cork bath mat)
- 1 metre (1¼yd) Vilene Ultrasoft iron-on interfacing

Method

Open out your fabric and fold across the bias grain (Fig 1). From the folded edge measure 25mm (1") wide strips across the whole fabric and cut out. Set these strips to one side. Do not join any of the bias strips as they will not slip through the trimming and tape maker.

Method for using the rotary cutter. Open out the fabric and fold on the bias grain (Fig 1), folding it again until the fabric is easy to handle (Fig 2). With your special cutting board, ruler and rotary cutter, cut the fabric into 25mm (1") wide strips and set aside.

Feed the fabric through the wide end of the tape maker and press the folded trim as it is pulled through (Fig 3). It will now measure 13mm (½")

wide. As you finish pressing each piece, wind it onto a cardboard cylinder to keep it smooth and straight until you are ready to start your weaving. Continue to press all the fabric strips winding them on to the cardboard cylinder as you progress.

Take the pattern of your front panel and cut a section of the iron-on interfacing 13mm (½") larger all round than your pattern and place this adhesive side up on your covered cork board. Do not cut out the shaping around the neckline – this will be done when the weaving is finished.

Mark your centre front line. Now mark your bias grain line (Fig 4).

Follow the instructions given on page 27 for the fabric and ribbon weaving technique.

When the weaving is complete (Fig 5), place your pattern onto your woven section matching up your grain lines, pin in place and cut around the pattern.

Machine all around this cut edge to hold the ribbons and fabric weaving in place. Your woven panel is now ready to use. Treat this panel in the same way as any other fabric for the dress adding interlining and lining.

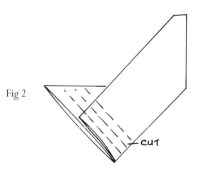

Fig 1

Fig 2

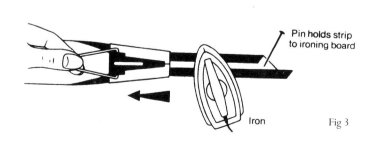

Pin holds strip to ironing board

Iron

Fig 3

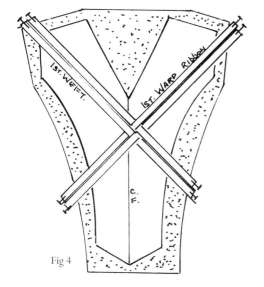

Fig 4

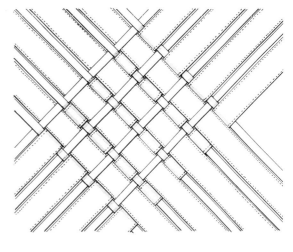

Fig 5

Follow the same procedure for the woven cuffs, marking your bias grain line for your first warp ribbon.

After months of meticulous planning the magic lasts for only one day, but the memories you shared will last a lifetime.

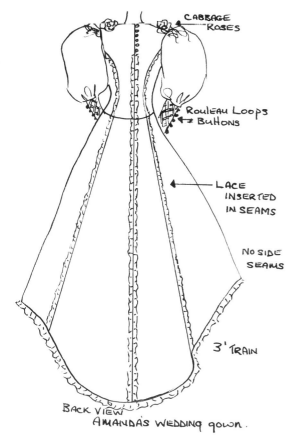

CABBAGE ROSES

ROULEAU LOOPS
& BUTTONS

LACE
INSERTED
IN SEAMS

NO SIDE
SEAMS

3' TRAIN

BACK VIEW
AMANDA'S WEDDING gown.

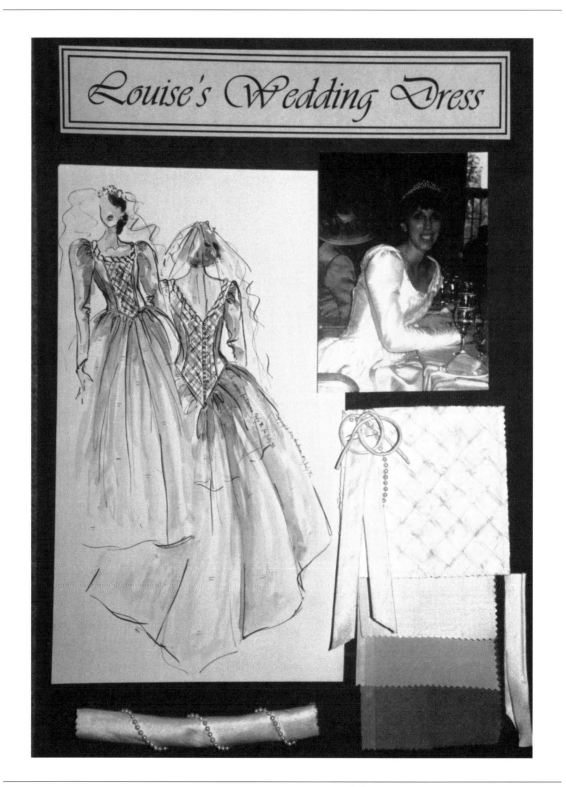

Louise's Wedding Dress

Louise's wedding dress

This beautiful wedding gown, made for my daughter-in-law Louise, with its Elizabethan-style neckline was immensely flattering to her tall slender shape. The centre front and the centre back panels of her dress were richly textured with fabric weaving, woven on the bias grain. The neckline was trimmed with a wide padded rouleau entwined with pearls, rouleau loops and self-covered buttons closed the centre back opening. The sleeve edges were shaped into a point towards the ring finger and trimmed with pearls. The lowered waistline was shaped to a point at the front and into a deep point at the centre back – this was emphasised with a corded rouleau onto a full gathered skirt. The long train was shaped into a point following the line of the back bodice. The fabric chosen for this gown was a closely woven pure silk dupion, lined with silk Habatia and interlined through out the entire gown with pure silk organza. This unseen layer of silk organza is vital to the look of the finished gown and nothing can be used as a substitute if you want a truly professional look.

The front bodice used one extra metre (1¼yd) of fabric, and the back bodice panels required an extra 1.5 metres (1¾yd) of 112cm (44") wide fabric.

Method – front bodice

Take one metre (1¼yd) of your fabric and fold on the bias, cut into 6cm (2¼") wide strips. Fold each strip in half lengthways, machine the width of the foot from the raw edges.

Turn through to the right side, press seam to one side, not down the centre. Cut your interfacing slightly larger than your bodice panels and place on the cork board adhesive side facing you. Mark the bias grain lines on the front bodice, pin first fabric strip along this line (Fig 1).

Continue to pin out the fabric strips until the bodice is covered.

To weave the warp strips (Fig 3), follow the instructions for the bias weave, press carefully when finished, place your pattern onto the weaving and cut out the bodice shape. Machine around the edge, just inside your seam allowance and press again. Your panel is now ready to use in your dress.

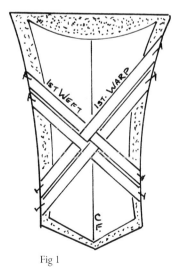

Fig 1

After weaving the first back panel (Fig 2), do not forget to reverse the pattern for the second panel. Alternatively, place both pieces of interfacing on the board together, centre backs facing each other and weave them simultaneously. By doing this you will ensure the grain line matches.

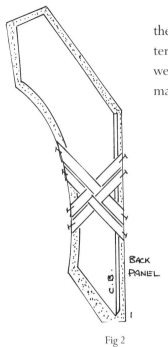

Fig 2

Fig 3

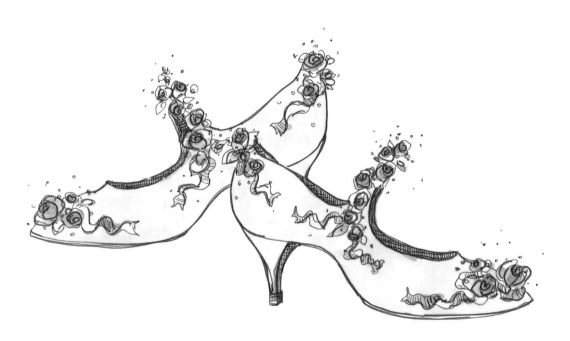

Wedding slippers

Ribbon and fabric roses have transformed a simple pair of satin shoes into a richly textured and elegant shoe, a dream for any bride to complete the fantasy right down to the tips of her toes. To decorate your own shoes you will need small pieces of your dress fabrics. I have used the silk dupion, organza and ribbon, making small folded and gathered roses stitched onto the covered and decorated wire you see illustrated below. Use the designs sketched here to transform any of your slippers or plain shoes into something special for cocktail or evening wear, or as shown here, for the bride.

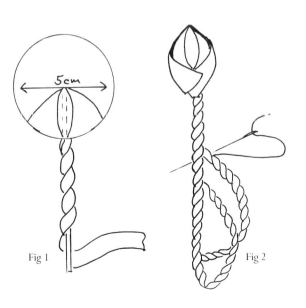

Materials

- 10cm (4") silk dupion
- 10cm (4") silk organza
- 2 metres (2yd 7") of 3mm (⅛") wide ribbon in wedding white
- 80cm (31½") of fine wire with a plastic coating, 40cm (16") for each shoe

Method

Cut the silk dupion into 1.5cm (½") strips on the bias and fold in half lengthways. Cover the wire by winding the fabric at an acute angle smoothing and stretching as you wind (Fig 1).

Make a small rosebud by cutting a circle of fabric 5cm (2") in diameter, fold in half (Fig 1) sandwich the covered wire, fold into centre to form a pointed cone shape, gather the cut edge around the wire and stitch into place.

Fold the covered wire to form two loops, secure with stitches at the centre (Fig 2).

Make two more buds the same as the first and sew in place (Fig 3).

Fig 1

5cm

Fig 2

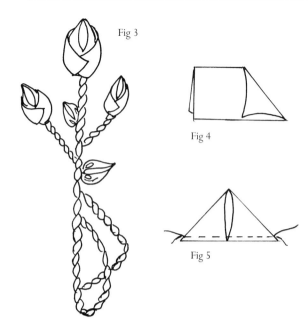

Fig 3

Fig 4

Fig 5

For the leaves, fold a 5cm (2") square of organza and one of dupion in half. Bring the folded ends to the centre (Fig 4). Make a row of gathering stitches along the raw edge (Fig 5) and sew in place on the covered wire.

Make several small cabbage roses in dupion and organza by taking a strip of fabric 2cm × 10cm (¾" × 4") wide, fold in half lengthways and follow the instructions for the roses on page 40.

Make three or four roses in various sizes and stitch them onto the covered wire making your own design and adding more leaves where necessary. Decorate with pearls and loops of the narrow ribbon and attach to the outside edge of each shoe.

This same combination of leaves and roses will look attractive made in black with gold ribbon for evening shoes.

More ideas to decorate your evening or special occasion shoes

- Sparkling evening shoes with fabric roses decorated with sequins and gold ribbon.
- Ballet slippers trimmed with ribbon roses and leaves.
- Black evening shoes decorated with gold ribbon and fabric roses attached with glue.
- Ribbon roses glued in place, decorated with pearls and sequins.

Evening purse

This lovely evening purse, with an optional plaited strap, is woven in fabric and ribbon using the bias weave with fabric made to match the evening gown. Two shades of narrow ribbon in clematis and violet were plaited together for the shoulder strap and woven with the shot silk taffeta for the purse. The weaving technique uses the tape maker, but you could substitute the fabric for the 13mm (½") wide ribbon if you wish. The fabric trim is used in the warp and in the weft. The narrow ribbon is used in the weft only.

Materials

- 🎀 50cm (20") of fabric, 112cm (44") wide (the fabric used here is shot silk taffeta)
- 🎀 6 metres (7½yd) double-faced satin ribbon, 3mm (⅛") wide in violet
- 🎀 3 metres (3¾yd) double-faced satin ribbon 3 mm (⅛" wide) in clematis
- 🎀 Vilene Ultrasoft iron-on interfacing 27cm × 40cm (10¾" × 15¾")
- 🎀 Canvas or pelmet Vilene 24cm × 38cm (9½" × 15")
- 🎀 Lining 39cm × 25cm (15½" × 10")
- 🎀 Velcro spot-ons for closure or magnetic clasp

- Trimming and tape maker, 12mm (½") wide.
- If you prefer to make the purse in ribbon only, you will need 20 metres (25yd) of 13mm (½") wide ribbon in single- or double-faced satin.
- Plaited strap (optional extra) – 1 metre 20cm (2yd) of violet 2 metre 40cm (4yd) of clematis
- Prepare the fabric strips following the instructions for the fabric weaving on page 27.

Method

Mark the bias centre in both directions onto the interfacing.

Warp – using only the fabric strips, pin out the warp starting from the grain line. Lay fabric strips side by side until the warp is complete and the interfacing covered (Fig 1).

Weft – starting from the grain line, weave *one violet ribbon, one clematis ribbon, one violet ribbon, two fabric strips* side by side.

Repeat from * to * until the weft is complete. Finish and press in the usual way. Trim to neaten the edges and machine around edge of rectangle to keep ribbons in place.

Making up the purse
Place the canvas or pelmet Vilene onto the wrong side of the woven panel. Fold the edges closely around the canvas on all four sides, hand sew in place (Fig 3).

Plaited strap – using the 3mm (⅛") wide ribbon, two clematis and one violet (1.20cm/½" long), make a three-strand plait (Fig 2). Machine the ends together to secure them. Hand stitch in place (Fig 3).

Fold in the seam allowance of the lining and press. Place over the canvas covering the raw edges of the woven panel and hand stitch in place (Fig 3).

Fold the purse up along the base fold line and hand sew a small gusset 2.5cm (1") wide between the front and back panel.

A magnetic clasp or velcro spot-ons can be used for the closure.

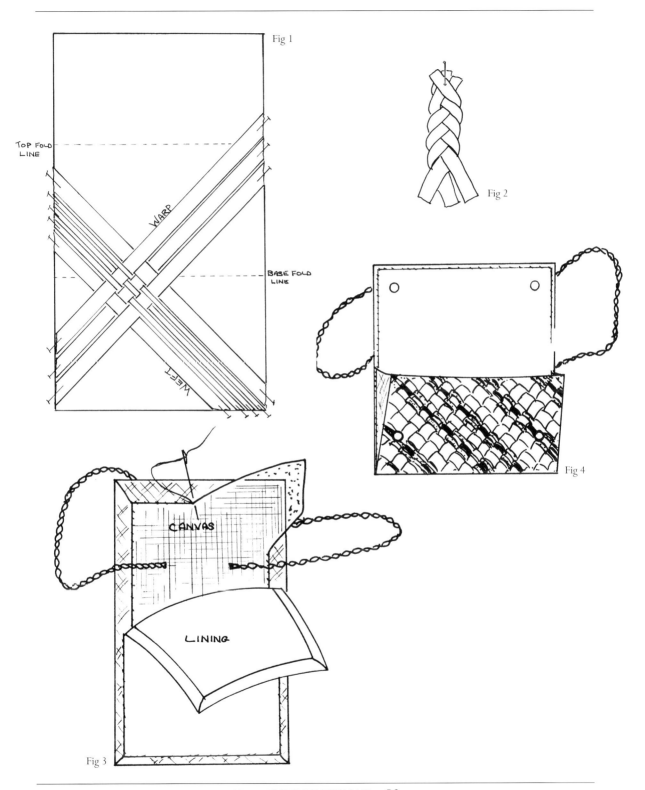

Fig 1

TOP FOLD
LINE

WARP

BASE FOLD
LINE

WEFT

Fig 2

Fig 4

CANVAS

LINING

Fig 3

Ribbon layered purse

This high fashion purse is made of polyester grosgrain ribbon stitched in over-lapping layers onto a matching background fabric. Both the grosgrain ribbons and the petersham ribbons are ideal for this purse as they are very hard wearing. A gilt chain with the grosgrain ribbon threaded through was used for the shoulder strap.

Materials

- Canvas for a stiff interfacing 25cm × 50cm (9¾" × 19¾")
- Lining 27cm × 52cm (10½" × 20½")
- Backing fabric 28cm × 54cm (11" × 21¼") navy blue wool crepe was used for this purse
- Vilene Ultrasoft iron-on interfacing 28cm × 54cm (11" × 21¼")
- 8 metres (9yd) of 25mm (1") wide grosgrain ribbon
- One metre (1¼yd) of gilt chain
- Gilt fastener (optional extra)
- Velcro spot-on for closure

Making up

Press the Vilene on to the wrong side of the backing fabric. Mark your seam allowance on the Vilene on all sides, 2cm (¾") on the top and bottom edge and 1.5cm (½") on each side. Place the canvas over the Vilene, inside the seam allowance and tack in place.

Working from the top edge which will become the front flap, place the first ribbon horizontally across the background fabric 4.5cm (1¾") in from the top edge = 2.5cm (1") above hemline and machine in place through the Vilene and canvas.

Machine the next ribbon in place by overlapping this ribbon by 6mm (¼"). Repeat this procedure until you have four ribbons in place (Fig 1).

Machine along both sides of the next four ribbons overlapping them in the same way. This is to keep the ribbons flat for the first fold.

Machine the next seven ribbons in the same design as the first four, but in the opposite direction. This is now the back of the purse.

Machine the next two ribbons along both edges – this is for the base of the purse.

Machine the next seven ribbons in the same direction and design as the first four.

Press all stitching carefully. Turn in seam allowance on all sides, hand stitch to the canvas.

Take one metre of the grosgrain ribbon, fold in half lengthways and top stitch, press, thread it through the gilt chain.

Place gilt chain in position 9cm (3½") in from each edge along the second fold line, stitch firmly

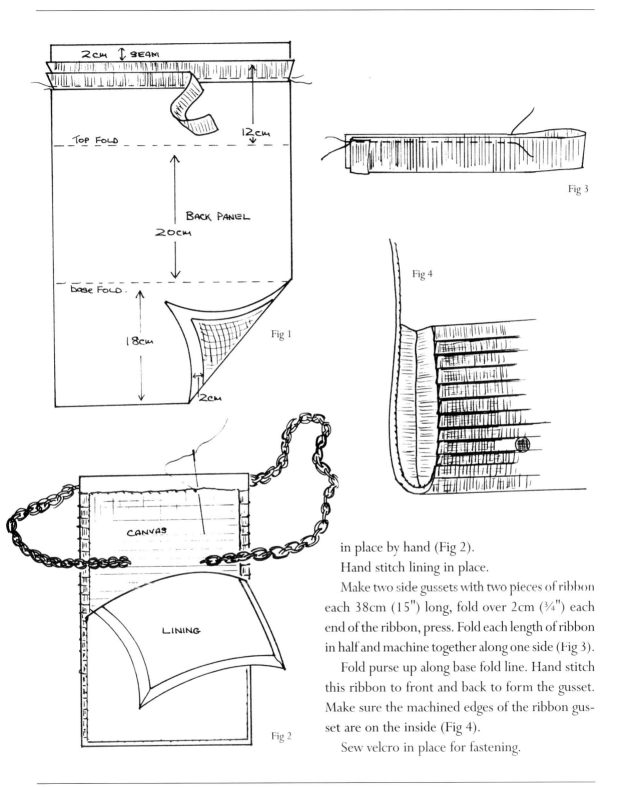

2cm ↕ SEAM

TOP FOLD

12cm

BACK PANEL

20cm

base FOLD.

18cm

2cm

Fig 1

Fig 3

Fig 4

CANVAS

LINING

Fig 2

in place by hand (Fig 2).

Hand stitch lining in place.

Make two side gussets with two pieces of ribbon each 38cm (15") long, fold over 2cm (¾") each end of the ribbon, press. Fold each length of ribbon in half and machine together along one side (Fig 3).

Fold purse up along base fold line. Hand stitch this ribbon to front and back to form the gusset. Make sure the machined edges of the ribbon gusset are on the inside (Fig 4).

Sew velcro in place for fastening.

Christening robe and bonnet

This exquisite christening robe and bonnet, made in pure silk dupion with its fabric and ribbon woven bodice and bonnet panel, is lavishly trimmed with pure silk Nottingham lace. I designed and made this robe as a family heirloom to be handed down in my family and used for many generations to come for both boys and girls. The robe and bonnet form part of my *Woven Treasure* collection which has sold in London, Norway, Los Angeles and France.

You could adapt this design for yourself by using a good commercial pattern and following the instructions for the plain weave for the bodice and bonnet panel, but using the fabric and ribbon weaving technique described for Amanda's wedding dress, using the trimming and tape maker.

The robe opens down the centre back (the French way) for easy access when handling babies and is fully lined throughout. The front panel is embellished with pin tucks and lace, repeated on the sleeves, a double row of wide lace trims the yoke, sleeves, hem and neckline. The bonnet is also lined throughout. The 3mm (⅛") wide double-faced satin ribbon was used in the woven panels and the 25mm (1") wide double-faced satin ribbon was used to tie the bonnet. The matching bootees are also lined in silk, trimmed with lace and have folded roses to decorate them.

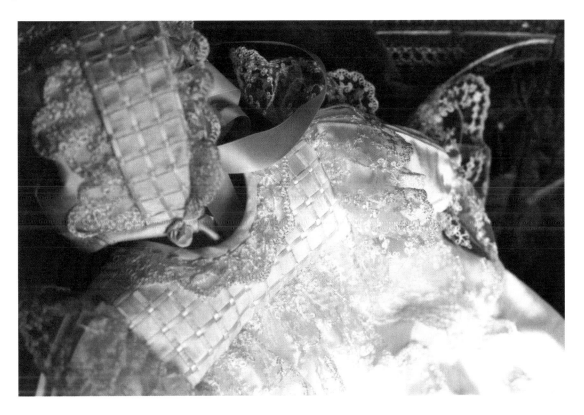

Christening suit

This lovely suit, especially designed and made for a baby boy, is made in a polyester satin fabric with ribbon weaving using the plain weave and mixing the 3mm (⅛") wide ribbon with the 13mm (½") wide ribbon. The bonnet panel is also made with this combination and trimmed with lace. The suit has trousers to the knee with short sleeves and a delightful pair of bootees tied with a large satin bow.

Dorothy bag

Materials

- The fabric for the Dorothy bag was made from the bride's wedding gown fabric.
- Two pieces of fabric 37.5cm × 21cm (14¾" × 8¼")
- Two circles of fabric 13cm (5") round
- One circle of stiff card for base 11cm (4¼") round
- Three sections of lace in various widths 38cm (15") long
- Decorative ribbon 38cm (15") long by 22mm (¾") wide
- Strip of Bondaweb for backing of ribbon
- One metre (1¼yd) of cord or ribbon for drawstring
- Matching thread to fabric
- These measurements include a 1cm (⅜") seam allowance.

Method

With the right side of the fabric facing you, measure 11cm (4¼") down from the top edge of the bag and place the wide section of lace in position. Pin and machine in place (Fig 1). Press.

Following the manufacturer's instructions, press the Bondaweb onto the back of the ribbon and position the ribbon over the edge of the lace. Press, then machine in place, press again.

Pin and machine the narrower sections of lace along the top and bottom edges of the bag. Press. On the top edge, **keep lace clear of seam allowance** by folding the lace back 1cm (⅜") from each edge (Fig 1).

Make a 1.5cm (½") buttonhole in the centre of the fabric, 5cm (2") from the top edge (Fig 1).

Place lining section over the main fabric, right sides facing, and machine together, following the machine line for the lace trim (Fig 2). Press machine stitching.

Fold fabric in half to form a tube, pin and machine seam together leaving part of the lining section open to turn through (Fig 3). Press seam open.

Mark circles into four sections by folding – do the same with both ends of the tubes (Fig 4). Place these balance marks together, pin and machine in place (Fig 5).

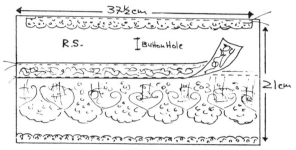

Fig 1

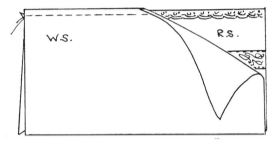

Fig 2

Turn to the right side through the side opening, place the stiffened base card in the base of the bag, hand stitch the open edges together.

With the right side facing you, mark down 4cm (1½") from the top edge and machine stitch around the bag. Mark a second row 6cm (2⅜") from the top edge and make a second row of stitching to form the casing for the ribbon. Carefully

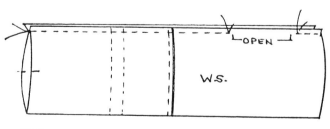

Fig 3

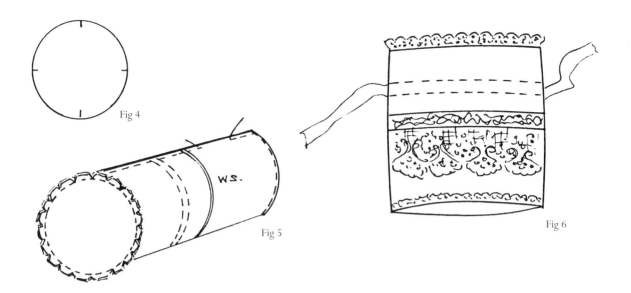

Fig 4

Fig 5

WS.

Fig 6

open the seam between the rows of stitching and thread a length of ribbon through this opening and a second ribbon through the buttonhole. Stitch the ends of each length of ribbon together to form a circle, pull the ribbon to hide the stitching inside the casing.

Special Gifts

Memories album

The stunning cover on this memories album is a simple way to decorate a large area with rich textures. A combination of ribbons and braids have been woven together in soft shades of ivory and beige and embellished with tassels, cords and roses. A 23cm (9") woven square was made and cut diagonally in half, with the sections placed in opposing corners. A rich corded trim was then added for further opulence to the beautiful panels. Two cords, one in ivory and one in beige, were twisted together to trim the outer edge (this is an optional extra).

This is an expanding album with the front cover being completely detachable – only the front was embellished, the back cover was left plain.

- 7 metres 10cm (7¾yd) double-faced satin ribbon, 3mm (⅛") wide in cream
- 5 metres (5½yd) braid, 8mm (¼") wide in beige
- 2 metres 20cm (2¾yd) braid, 8mm (¼") wide in ivory
- 2 metres 50cm (3yd) of decorative cord trimming
- 1 metre 50cm (2yd) of ivory and beige cord twisted together for the edging (optional)
- Vilene Ultrasoft iron-on interfacing 23cm (9") square
- Glass-headed pins

- Covered cork board
- 4oz wadding cut to exact size of the cover
- Piece of backing fabric same size as wadding – muslin or organza is fine
- Enough background fabric to fit both sides of your front cover. The finished cover here measures 32cm (12¾") square. An extended seam allowance was left on to the left side of this album. Silk dupion was used for this cover with a 2cm (¾") seam allowance being allowed all around as this fabric frays.

Method

Follow the directions for the plain weave and proceed as follows.

Warp – cut the beige braid into twenty-two, 23cm (9") lengths. Cut the ivory braid into nine, 23cm (9") lengths. Cut the 3mm (⅛") wide ribbon into nineteen, 23cm (9") lengths.

Starting from the centre, pin in sequence, one ribbon, one ivory braid, one ribbon, one beige braid, one ribbon. Repeat this sequence until the warp is complete.

Weft – using only the beige braid and ribbon, starting from the centre weave across in sequence, one ribbon, one braid, one ribbon, until the weft is complete.

It is this narrow ribbon woven between each braid plus the ivory braid in the warp only, that produces this subtle but opulent texture. Ensure the narrow ribbon starts and finishes on all four sides of your weaving. When the weaving is pressed and finished cut the weaving diagonally in half, machine around the edges of the diagonal on all three sides. Press again.

Place the cover of your album onto the fabric and mark the edges around this with a marker pen or by tacking. Mark a 2cm (¾") seam allowance on three sides and 2.5cm (1") on the left-hand side. Do the same with the lining and cut them out.

Place the wadding onto the wrong side of your top fabric inside your seam allowance, place backing fabric (not the lining) over the wadding and tack in position through all three layers.

With the right side of top fabric facing you, place one woven panel in the top right-hand corner just

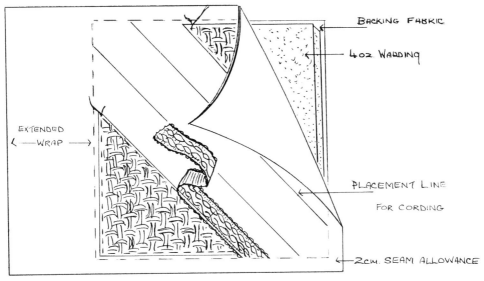

BACKING FABRIC

4 oz WADDING

EXTENDED
← WRAP →

PLACEMENT LINE

FOR CORDING

2 cm. SEAM ALLOWANCE

Fig 1

inside the seam allowance and the other in the bottom left-hand corner, pin and machine in place through all thicknesses (Fig 1).

Place a length of the flat cording along the inner edges of the woven panels to cover the machine stitches, machine or hand sew in position (Fig 1). Place two other lengths of cording parallel to the panels and sew in place by hand or machine (fabric glue could be used instead of hand sewing).

With the right sides together place the lining panel over the decorative work, following the markings for the seam allowance, pin and machine in place on three sides only, leave open the left-hand side. Press machine stitching.

Trim seams, turn through to the right side and fit the cover over the album. Starting on your left-hand side place the corded trim all around the edge of the album (Fig 2) making sure you cover the raw edges of the woven panels as you proceed. Butt the

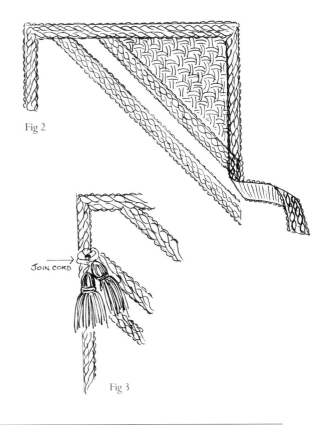

Fig 2

JOIN CORD

Fig 3

two ends of the cord together for a smooth finish and dab with fray check to eliminate fraying. Hand stitch the cord in place, or to save time, use a good fabric glue to hold the cord in place.

Make two ribbon roses and place over the join in the cording, add the tassels and stitch in place under the roses. An additional cord was used to edge the album illustrated – this was done by twisting two cords together and gluing them in place around the edge.

Bible jacket

This beautiful ribbon woven jacket cover trimmed with Nottingham lace was made to cover a bible. It makes a lovely enduring gift for little bridesmaids to treasure as well as a marvellous christening present. The bible chosen for this gift was a silver-edged presentation edition, measuring 15cm × 10cm (5¾" × 4").

The instructions given here are for a jacket cover, 23cm × 15cm (9" × 6") finished measurement.

Materials

- 5 metres (5½yd) double-faced satin ribbon, 3mm (⅛") wide in white
- 5 metres (5½yd) single-faced satin ribbon, 10mm (⅜") wide in white
- Vilene Ultrasoft iron-on interfacing measuring 18cm × 26cm (7" × 10¼")
- 25cm (9¾") of a jacquard ribbon for the bookmark
- Lining for the side pockets, two pieces each measuring 16cm × 19cm (6¼" × 7½")
- Lining for centre section – one piece measuring 16cm × 11cm (6¼" × 4¼")
- One metre (1¼yd) of narrow lace

Method

Following the instructions for the plain weave use the weaving sequence, one 10mm (⅜") wide ribbon, one 3mm (⅛") wide ribbon in both the warp and the weft to produce the quilted look. When the weaving is complete trim it to measure 24cm × 16cm (9½" × 6¼"), machine all around the weaving 6mm (¼") in from the edge. Press.

With the right side of weaving facing you, place the narrow lace all around the edge of the woven panel and machine in place (Fig 1). Add the ribbon ties 14cm (5½") long.

Fold the lining for the side panels in half and place one section each side of the woven panel, folded edges towards the centre, right sides facing.

Place the jacquard ribbon down the centre of the panel, right sides together.

Machine a 6mm (¼") single seam either side of the centre panel section and place in position down the centre over the side panels (Fig 2).

Machine panels in place. For accurate stitching, turn your work to the reverse side and follow the

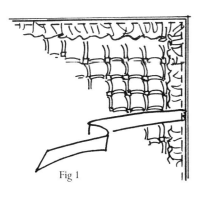

Fig 1

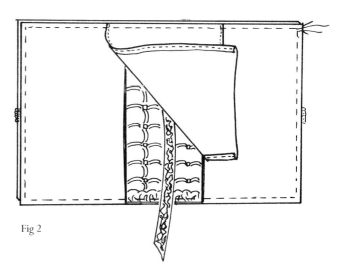

Fig 2

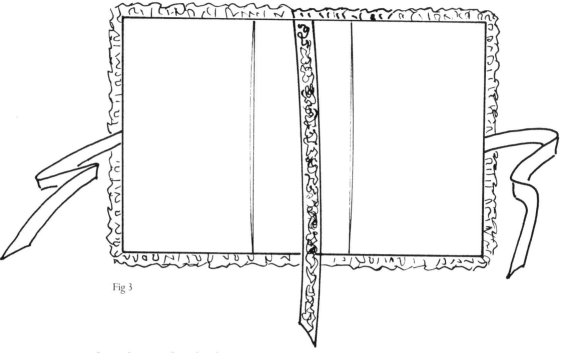

Fig 3

previous row of machining for the lace. Press
machine stitching carefully. Turn through to the
right side (Fig 3).

Fit woven jacket onto the bible (Fig 4).

Fig 4

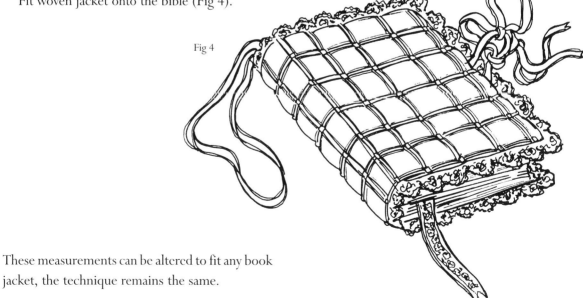

These measurements can be altered to fit any book
jacket, the technique remains the same.

Needle case

This small Victorian needle case would be ideal as a first sampler. It would also make an excellent class project or a beautiful gift to give to anyone who sews.

Materials

- 4 metres (4½yd) single-faced satin ribbon, 10mm (⅜") wide in claret
- 1.60cm (1yd 27") double-faced satin ribbon, 3mm (⅛") wide in purple
- 1.60cm (1yd 27") gold lurex ribbon, 3mm (⅛") wide
- 60cm (23½") of fine gold cord trim
- Thick designer tacky glue
- Section of Vilene Ultrasoft iron-on interfacing for weaving 14cm × 17cm (5½" × 6¾")
- Stiff card for the backing measuring 10cm × 13cm (4" × 5")
- Thin layer of wadding 10cm × 13cm (4" × 5")
- Section of lining 13cm × 15cm (5" × 6")
- Felt for the pins 9cm × 10cm (3½" × 4")
- Covered cork board for weaving
- Glass-headed pins

Follow instructions for the plain weave, pinning out ribbons as follows.

Warp ribbons – starting in the centre, pin out one red ribbon, one gold ribbon side by side across the warp until you have a total of 11 red ribbons and 10 gold ribbons in the warp.

Weft ribbons – starting in the centre, weave one purple ribbon, one red ribbon until you have woven a total of 10 red ribbons and 9 purple ribbons in the weft.

When the weaving is complete, follow the instructions for the plain weave to finish and press, ready for making into the needle case. Trim weaving to measure 13cm × 15.5cm (5" × 6") and machine 6mm (¼") in from the edge.

Score the stiff card down the fold line (Fig 1) place a line of glue around the edges, place the layer of wadding onto the card over the glue, cut the wadding down the fold line to match exactly the scored line on the card, leave to dry.

With the scored side out place the ribbon woven panel onto the card over the wadding, folding over the 12mm (½") seam allowance, glue in place (Fig 2).

Cut two ribbon ties 25cm (10") long from the red ribbon and glue in place 2cm (¾") in from the edge (Fig 2).

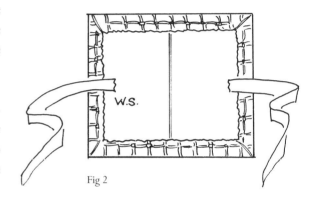

Fig 2

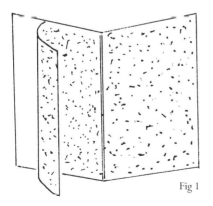

Fig 1

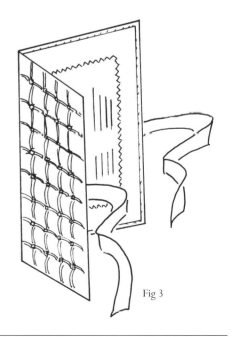

Fig 3

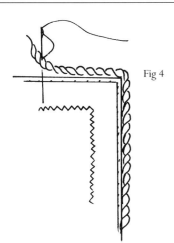

Fig 4

Turn in seam allowance around the edge of the lining section and press. Pin lining carefully in place covering the raw edges of ribbon on the wrong side, hand sew in place.

Position the felt in centre of the needle case (Fig 3), place a spot of glue along centre fold of felt to hold it in place.

Hand stitch the gold cord in place around the edge of the needle case, tuck the ends of the cord inside the lining (Fig 4).

Spectacle holder

You will never lose your glasses again with this delightful holder to keep them safe. Made in the simple plain weave to the same weaving design as the needle case, by adding the Russia braid and a fancy tassel, it makes a lovely decoration to wear around your neck.

Materials

- 5 metres (5½yd) satin ribbon, 10mm (⅜") wide in claret
- 3 metres (3¼yd) gold lamé, 3mm (⅛") wide
- 3 metres (3¼yd) double-faced satin ribbon, 3mm (⅛") wide in purple
- 20cm square (8") Vilene Ultrasoft iron-on interfacing
- 20cm square (8") of lining fabric
- 80cm (32") of Russia braid
- Tassel

Method

Following the instructions for the plain weave and the weaving sequence for the needle case, make a 17cm × 20cm (7" × 8") section of weaving.

Using the pattern produced here, Fig 1 (each square represents 1cm/⅜") cut out the spectacle holder from the woven panel. Machine around the edge of the shape to hold the ribbons in place. Cut out the lining section using the same pattern.

With the right sides together, place the lining section over the woven panel and machine together along the top edge only (Fig 2). Understitch to hold the lining in place. Press. Fold lining to the inside.

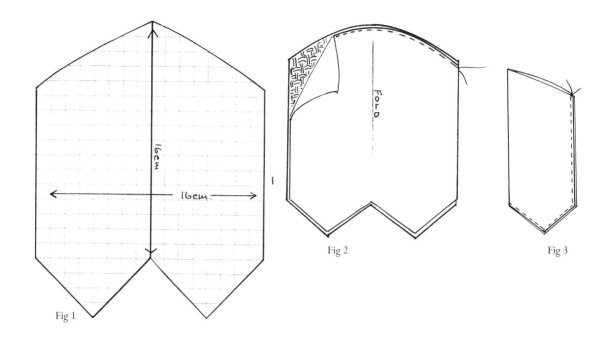

Fig 1

Fig 2

Fig 3

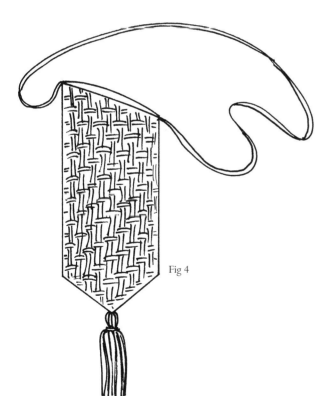

Fig 4

Place the tassel loop at the centre of the point and pin in place on the right side. With right sides together, fold the case in half, pin and machine together down the side and around the point, being careful to keep the tassel at the centre of the point (Fig 3). You may find a cording foot helpful when machining around the point.

Turn through to the right side and press carefully (Fig 4).

Attach the Russia braid by hand, sewing it just inside the folded and seamed edge (Fig 4).

Scissors holder

This delightful little scissors holder made from 50mm (2¼") wide velvet ribbon makes a pretty case to store your scissors in. It takes less than an hour to make and can be embellished as simply or as richly as you wish.

Materials

- 35cm (13¾") velvet ribbon, 50mm (2¼") wide
- 1 metre (1¼yd) Russia braid in matching colour to ribbon
- Tassels in two sizes
- 50cm (20") of 3mm (⅛") wide ribbon to tie to the scissors
- Roses to decorate flap
- Fabric glue

Method

Cut velvet ribbon into two sections measuring 21cm (8¼") and 14cm (5½").

Following the diagram in Fig 1, make a flat point at one end of both ribbon sections and glue in place.

Make a second point on the opposite end of the longer piece of ribbon following the diagram in Figs 1 and 2, and placing the smaller tassel in this second fold.

On the shorter section fold over the top edge by 2cm (¾") and glue in place. Attach the larger tassel on to the pointed end.

With the wrong side facing you, place a fine line of glue along the three outer edges on the smaller section of ribbon. Place this over the larger piece of ribbon, being careful to match the two points together.

Attach the cord under the flap. Tie the narrow ribbon to the scissors and sew in place at the side of the holder.

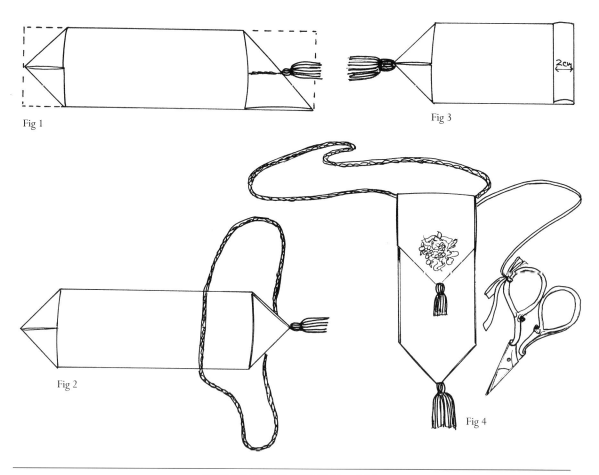

Fig 1

Fig 3

Fig 2

Fig 4

Bookmark

Every book deserves a lovely bookmark and this one is simple and quick to make. It would make an ideal project for a young person to make as a gift for parents or friends for birthdays or Christmas. One metre (1¼yd) of 50mm (2¼") wide ribbon makes four bookmarks. Alternatively, if you wish to make it double, 41cm (16") will make one bookmark.

Materials

- 1 metre (1¼yd) velvet 50mm (2¼") wide
- 50cm (20") of 10mm (⅜") wide satin ribbon for the roses, or one packet of ready made roses
- Fabric glue
- Small tassel

Method

Cut the velvet ribbon into four equal lengths. Fold bottom edge of ribbon diagonally (Fig 1) and place the tassel in the centre, glue in position. Fold across again to form a point (Fig 2). Fold 2cm (¾") over once at the top edge and glue in place. On the right side of the bookmark, make ribbon roses and glue in place.

If you wish to make the double-sided bookmark, fold the top edge over 1cm (⅜"). Fold this edge down to meet the lower edge, butt edges together and glue in place (Fig 3).

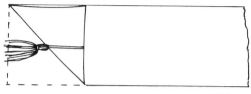

Fig 1

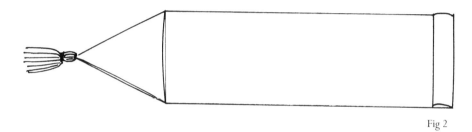

Fig 2

Fig 3   Double layer bookmark

Correspondence folder

A correspondence folder makes a beautiful gift for someone special for both birthdays and Christmas. It is simple and quick to make, and the only sewing involved is to machine the two ribbons together. The folder is made in a strong quality jacquard fabric and decorated with the picot-edged petersham ribbon onto which a beautiful jacquard ribbon has been bonded for easy handling. The folder is then tied together with a second jacquard ribbon.

Materials

- Cardboard – 2mm (⅛") thick, 2 sections 22cm × 30cm (8½" × 12") plus 2 outside sections 9cm × 29cm (3½" × 11½")
- Cardboard for side panels (240g) 9cm × 29cm (3½" × 11½").

Fabric for outer panels is in a quality furnishing weight:

- 2 sections 34cm × 26cm (13½" × 10")
- 2 sections 13cm × 33cm (5" × 13")
- 1 piece for spine 10cm × 36cm (4" × 14")
- Fabric for lining (a strong cotton was used):
- 1 section 33cm × 47cm (13" × 18½")
- 1 sheet of cartridge paper 29cm × 43cm (11½" × 17")

Ribbon trimmings:

- 80cm (31½") of picot-edged petersham for side trim, cut in two pieces
- 80cm (31½") of jacquard ribbon for side trim, cut in two pieces
- 40cm (16") of picot-edged petersham for top and bottom edge trim, cut in two pieces
- 40cm (16") of jacquard ribbon for top and bottom edge trim, cut in two pieces
- 60cm (23½") of 13mm (½") wide jacquard ribbon for the ties, cut in two pieces
- Fabric glue
- Pencil and ruler
- Heavy duty craft knife, scissors, cutting board and Bondaweb

Method

Cut cardboard and fabric to above measurements. Paint a thin film of glue over one side of both the pieces of the 2mm (⅛") thick cardboard.

Place the two outside sections of fabric flat on the table, side by side.

Carefully position the glued side of the card on to the fabric, leaving a 2cm (¾") fabric overlap on all four sides (Fig 1).

Trim the four corners at an angle to within 2mm (⅛") of card and carefully paint a thin layer of glue on the extended fabric. Fold the fabric over the edge of the card (Fig 1) and press in place with your fingers. Turn card over and smooth out any wrinkles you may have made. Repeat for second section.

Cover both sections of the 240g card in exactly

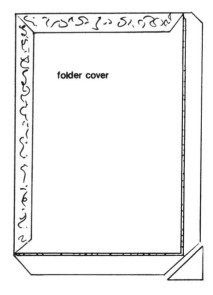

folder cover

Fig 1

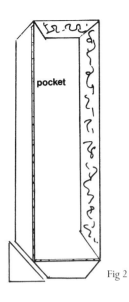

Fig 2

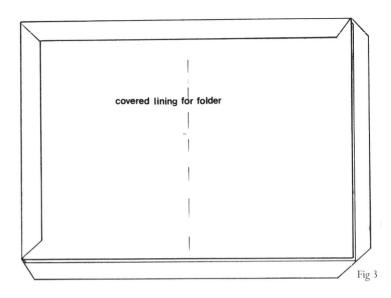

covered lining for folder

Fig 3

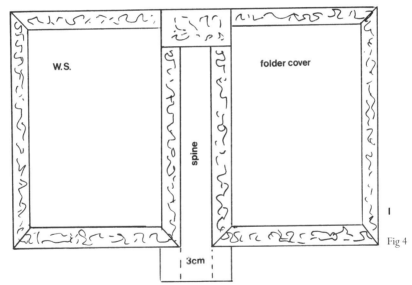

W.S.

spine

folder cover

3cm

Fig 4

the same way. Keep to one side (inside pocket sections). (Fig 2)

Cover the heavy duty cartridge paper in the same way, keep to one side for lining. (Fig 3)

To form the spine of your folder, place the spine fabric on the table with the wrong side facing you and measure in from each side 3.5cm (1½") and 3cm (1¼") from the top and bottom edge, draw a line along these points and lightly glue all around the edges.

Place your outside sections carefully in position, making sure they are parallel to each other with a

3cm (1¼") gap between them. Press in position with your hand. Fold remaining fabric over top and bottom edge, press again (Fig 4).

Bonding ribbons
Follow instructions on your Bondaweb packet and bond jacquard ribbon onto picot-edged petersham ribbon. Press (Fig 5).

Place one strip 40cm (15¾") of double ribbon over the raw edge of the spine fabric 2cm (¾") in from the fold, carefully glue in position and fold over 5cm (2") top and bottom. Smooth out any bubbles with your hand. Repeat over the second raw edge on the back of the folder (Fig 6).

Place the two 20cm (8") lengths of double ribbon over the corners on top and bottom of your

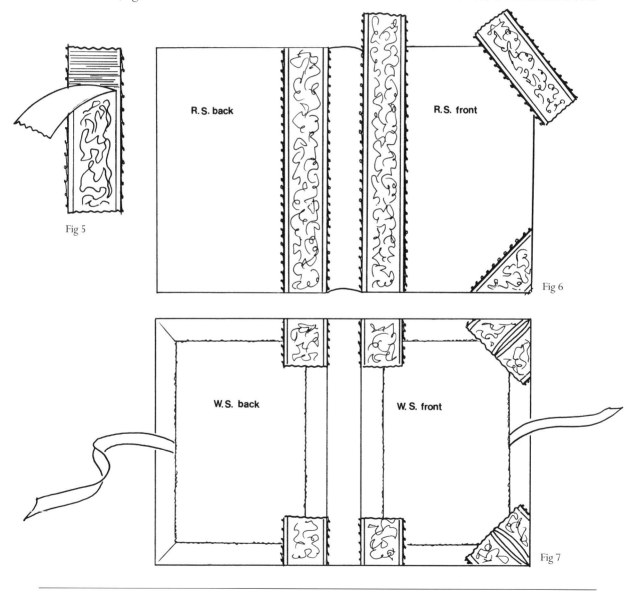

Fig 5

R.S. back

R.S. front

Fig 6

W.S. back

W.S. front

Fig 7

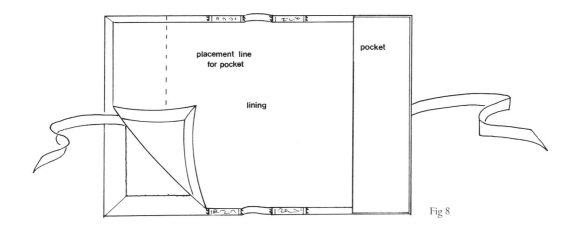

placement line
for pocket

pocket

lining

Fig 8

front folder. Glue carefully in place and fold ribbons over the wrong side and glue again (Fig 6).

To anchor your tying ribbons, place folder with the inside facing you and glue the ribbon 15cm (6") down from top edge and 2cm (¾") in from edge to anchor them well.

Spread glue carefully over lining and place over the inside of the folder. Press with your hands, making sure everything looks neat and tidy (Fig 8).

To fix inside pockets, carefully glue 1cm (⅜") in on 3 sides (two short sides and one long edge) and place pocket in position very close to the three outside edges on both the back and front of folder. Press carefully with your hand. Make sure your ribbons for tying are laid out flat. Leave folder opened out flat until dry under a heavy weight.

Desk diary

Decorate a plain black desk diary and turn it into a special gift for a friend at Christmas time. To do this you will need lining for the inside cover and ribbon for the bookmark plus ribbons for the decoration. For the diary shown on page 117 I have used the picot-edged petersham with a jacquard ribbon.

Method

Bond the petersham ribbon and the jacquard ribbon together, place along the left-hand side of the diary and glue in place. Do the same across both corners. Cut a piece of card the size of the inside cover of your diary and cover in an attractive lining using the fabric glue. Place the lining panel over the inside of the diary to cover the raw edges of the ribbon. Place the jacquard bookmark under the lining in the top right-hand corner.

Greetings cards

Hand-made greetings cards are always a pleasure to receive, and once you have mastered the rose making and weaving techniques in this book, you will be able to delight your friends with these lovely cards on special occasions in their lives.

Materials

- Greeting card blanks – double-folded cards with pre-cut apertures
- One piece of pure silk Habotia to fit the card
- Thin layer of wadding, slightly larger than the aperture

- Assorted ribbons
- Hand sewing needle
- Matching thread to ribbons
- Glue – Prit and UHU
- Small piece of Vilene Ultrasoft iron-on interfacing for the basket design card

Method

Cut a piece of the pure silk for the background, 7mm (¼") smaller than the card.

Cut the wadding to fit the aperture.

Check the card is in the right position, then draw through the aperture to the back of the card.

Open out the card, place the wadding over the drawn line and glue in place with the Prit.

Place the silk on top of the wadding and glue down on all sides with the UHU glue. Check there are no raw edges showing. Please note: **the silk is only placed on top of the wadding when you have completed the design**.

Place glue all around the inside of the centre section, fold over the padded section making sure the two surfaces are glued firmly together so that the wadded area is now backed by the front part of the card.

Your card is now ready to decorate in any design you wish. Make sure your card is in the correct position before you begin.

Basket of roses

Following the plain weave ribbon weaving instructions, make a small woven section in 3mm (⅛") wide ribbon in two shades.

Press Bondaweb on the back of the weaving, draw the shape of a basket onto the Bondaweb and cut out the shape. Peel the paper backing away from the Bondaweb. Press this woven basket shape very carefully into place on your card.

Using the same ribbons used for the basket, cut the two colours into 9cm (3½") lengths, twist them together and glue them in place so that the roses can be arranged under it and over the base of the handle.

Make a selection of tiny roses from various colours and textures of ribbon, using the 7mm (¼") and 10mm (⅜") wide ribbon and glue in place.

Decorate with small leaves. These must be cut at an angle from the ribbon to eliminate fraying. You could, of course, cheat a little with the tiny roses and buy the ready made variety, but the ones on the cards shown here are all hand made using the 10mm (⅜") wide ribbon.

Christmas candle

Cut a length of ribbon 8cm long × 22mm wide (3¼" × ¾") to represent the candle.

Cut a strip of Bondaweb the exact size of the ribbon and press onto the back of it. Peel off the paper when cold and press into place on your fabric.

Cut a flame shape in three graduating sizes, two in gold and one in red ribbon. Use the Bondaweb again to press into place at the top of the candle. Decorate the candle by placing three strips of 3mm (⅛") wide ribbon across it and press into place as before. Decorate the sides and base of the candle with roses made from the 10mm (⅜") wide ribbon. Add leaf shapes cut at an angle in two shades of green using 6mm (¼") ribbon.

Wedding bells

Draw a bell shape onto a piece of Bondaweb and press onto your chosen fabric. Peel away the backing paper and press onto your prepared silk.

Twist 13cm (5") of 3mm (⅛") wide ribbon into a bow and stick at the top of the bells. Place Russia braid around the bell shape and glue in position.

Make nine small ribbon roses and place around the top of the bells, add leaf shapes cut at an angle using the 6mm (¼") wide ribbon.

Ribbon ring

Cut 13cm (5") of 3mm (⅛") wide ribbon in two colours and twist into a bow. Place at the bottom of your prepared piece of silk and glue in place.

Make ten small ribbon roses in various soft colours and place them to form a ring, glue in position.

Twist a piece of Russia braid around and between the roses.

Cut leaf shapes in a variety of ribbons and two sizes. The ones used here are in gold lamé, organdie and satin.

Ribbon bags

Ribbon bags are a beautiful and luxurious way to gift wrap small presents to special friends. They look lovely decorating the Christmas table and can be used instead of the traditional Christmas cracker or as a little extra surprise when your guests and family sit down for lunch. Children love to open them to find a small present inside and a gift for adults is always a delight to receive.

There are two designs illustrated here. The first design uses the rich velvet ribbon and gold organdie ribbon top stitched together while the second design is made in the 75mm (3") wide ribbon and top stitched at the sides only. Both of these designs look lovely decorating the Christmas tree or you can fill the ribbon bags with pot-pourri, place them in a basket or dish to perfume your room.

Materials for striped bag

🎀 60cm (23½") of 25mm (1") wide red velvet ribbon

🎀 30cm (11¾") of 35mm (1½") wide gold striped organdie ribbon

🎀 Matching sewing thread to velvet ribbon

Method

Cut velvet ribbon in half and place one section down the edge of the organdie ribbon, machine together with a small zig-zag stitch. Repeat this sewing procedure with the second piece of velvet ribbon down the opposite side of the organdie ribbon, overlapping the ribbons very slightly (Fig 1).

Fold in half and zig-zag the open sides together. Trim top edge with pinking shears. Place your gift inside and tie with a bow in gold or red ribbon.

These ribbon bags look wonderful made in black and gold for a sophisticated dinner party and can be made to any size depending on the width of the ribbon used.

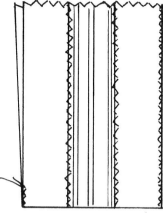

Fig 1

Materials for the plain bag

- 🎀 1 metre (1¼yd) of 75mm (3") wide ribbon. This will make 3 ribbon bags
- 🎀 1 metre 20cm (47") of 13mm (½") wide gold ribbon, to tie and decorate the 3 bags
- 🎀 Matching thread to ribbon

Method

Cut the wide ribbon into three equal lengths. Fold ends of ribbon over 1cm (⅜") then again to 3cm (1¼") (Fig 1). Press. With folded edges facing each other, fold in half and machine by top stitching together starting 2cm (¾") down from top edge just catching in the folded top.

Place your gift or pot-pourri in the bag and tie the neck with the contrasting ribbon.

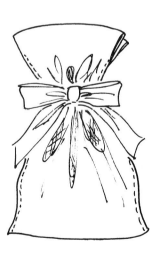

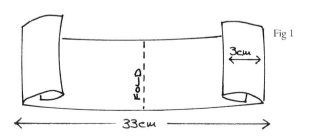

Fig 1

3cm

FOLD

33cm

Christmas stocking

This elaborate Christmas stocking is a delight to behold and would make a lovely gift for a special friend. The stocking is made in rich purple velvet, with a shaped cuff woven in ivory and gold ribbon. The edge of the stocking is trimmed with a gold and purple cord with gold tassels hanging from the pointed cuff.

Materials

- Velvet 40cm deep × 60cm wide (16" × 23½")
- 5 metres (5½yd) satin ribbon, 10mm (⅜") wide in ivory
- 5 metres (5½yd) gold lamé ribbon, 3mm (⅛") wide
- 70cm (27½") of 38mm (1½") wide metallic organdie wire-edged ribbon for the bow
- 40cm (16") of 3mm (⅛") wide gold lamé for the small bows
- Narrow gold braid across toe
- Strip of lining 10cm (4") deep for the inside boot top band
- 20cm (8") square of Vilene Ultrasoft iron-on interfacing
- 20cm (8") square of lining for the woven panel
- Two large gold tassels

Method

Cut out the velvet boot to the pattern shape. Each square represents half a centimetre 0.5cm (¼") (Fig 1). This pattern is one-quarter of the finished boot.

Machine gold braid in place across the toe.

Make up a 20cm (8") square of ribbon weaving using the gold and ivory ribbons and the interfacing, following the plain weave instructions.

Cut the woven panel and the lining in half on the diagonal, machine around the edges of the woven panel to keep ribbon in place (Fig 2).

With right sides together place lining over the woven panels and machine stitch along two sides, trim, turn to right side and press (Fig 3).

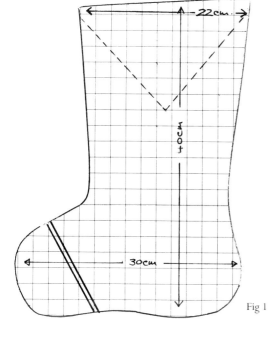

Fig 1

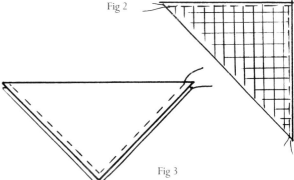

Fig 2

Fig 3

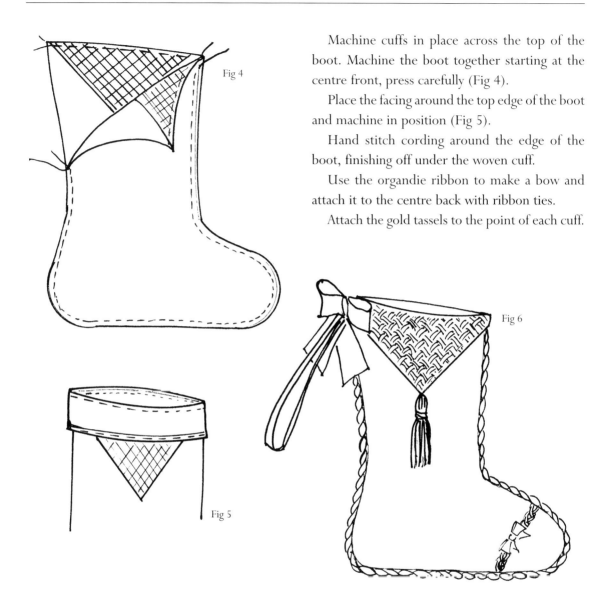

Machine cuffs in place across the top of the boot. Machine the boot together starting at the centre front, press carefully (Fig 4).

Place the facing around the top edge of the boot and machine in position (Fig 5).

Hand stitch cording around the edge of the boot, finishing off under the woven cuff.

Use the organdie ribbon to make a bow and attach it to the centre back with ribbon ties.

Attach the gold tassels to the point of each cuff.

Fig 4

Fig 5

Fig 6

Tissue holder

A small tissue holder for your purse is an ideal gift to give to friends or family at any time of the year. To make this gift a little more special for your wedding, you could make it from the fabric of the bride's dress or from the groom's waistcoat – it would make an ideal present for any special people who were unable to attend your wedding.

Materials

- One piece of fabric 33cm × 16cm (13" × 6¼")
- Decorative ribbon 32cm long × 22mm wide (12½" × 8½")
- Matching thread to ribbon
- Small packet of tissues 12cm × 6cm (4¾" × 2⅜")
- Strip of Bondaweb the length of the ribbon

Fold fabric in half and machine seam (Fig 1).

Place the seam to the centre of the fabric and press seam open (Fig 2). Leave top and bottom edges open.

Turn through to the right side and press folded edges flat.

Press the Bondaweb onto the ribbon following the manufacturer's instructions and trim to fit the ribbon.

Cut the length of ribbon in half, and with the right side of the tissue holder facing you, place the two sections of ribbon along the folded edges. Press the ribbon carefully into position, then machine in place. Press stitching (Fig 3).

Fold the ribboned edges, wrong side facing you, into the centre. Machine across both raw edges. Trim and neaten seams with a zig-zag stitch. Press stitching (Fig 4).

Turn through to the right side and fill with tissues.

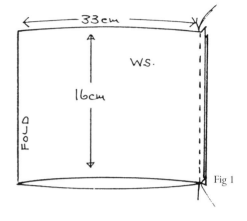

Fig 1

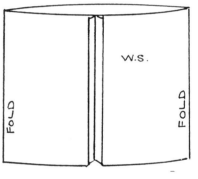

Fig 2

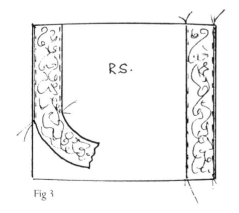

Fig 3

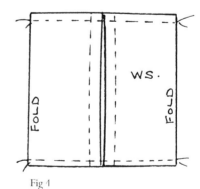

Fig 4

From the Designer's Sketch Pad

Lots of fashion illustrations for you to use and adapt

All the designs sketched here incorporate the various techniques described in this book. Using this knowledge and coupled with a good commercial pattern of your choice, you will be able to personalise your own garments making them truly original.

Jacket detail

The detail on the back of this ivory jacket is made with 7mm (¼") wide gold lamé ribbons woven in to the plain weave, the weaving is then cut in to a triangle. Bondaweb is pressed onto the back of the weaving and the weaving is then placed on the back of the jacket, pressed and machined in place. Gold braid 13mm (½") wide was applied first across the top edge of the weaving, then inserted into the shoulder seam and machined in place along the edge of the weaving. A large fat tassel was added for extra detail.

Tassel trim

Tassels make a charming and simple decoration on a sleeve creating interest, movement and rich texture. To create this texture you will need fusible 2oz wadding H640 by Vilene, 3mm (⅛") wide ribbon or Russia braid and tassels. The fusible wadding is first pressed onto the wrong side of the sleeve fabric, the Russia braid or narrow ribbon is then top stitched in place through the wadding and the tassels sewn on by hand. This design would also look wonderful with folded roses in place of the tassels.

Woven sleeve trim

Take a plain simple jacket sleeve and make it special by adding a diamond shape of weaving. To do this, draw the design onto the sleeve pattern, trace off the shape and use this as the pattern for the ribbon weaving section. When the weaving is complete use Bondaweb to place the woven section in position, trim with braid, machine in place and add the tassel.

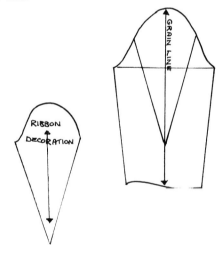

Cocktail dress

This sensational cocktail dress with its richly embellished back detail would be a hit at any party. Three different techniques are needed to interpret this design. The open bias weaving across the back is woven with lengths of matching rouleau, the plain weave at the waistline is woven in 7mm (¼") wide ribbon and the large folded roses are made in the 35mm (1") wide satin ribbon.

Long shirt

This long shirt with split sides, has stunning detail on the shoulder yoke and cuff created by the fabric and ribbon weaving technique. The pattern is adapted from a basic jacket pattern by adding the length you require, usually to 5cm (2") above the knee. A shoulder yoke was created and a 7cm wide (2¾") cuff was added to the sleeve pattern. The shoulder yoke and cuff require an extra ¾ metre (30") of your chosen fabric plus 10 metres (11yd) of 3mm (⅛") wide double-faced satin ribbon.

Cut the fabric into 5cm (2") wide strips on the straight grain. Fold in half lengthways and stitch 1cm (⅜") in from the raw edges. Turn strips through to the right side and press with the seam to one side. Do not trim as this extra fabric gives the strips a soft quilted effect when completed. Follow the instructions for the bias weave, starting at the centre of your yoke and cuff and weave with the fabric and ribbon. Do not cut away the interfacing from the neck shape until the weaving is complete. This design would look equally good for evening or daytime wear.

Party dress

This fascinating back has a net insert for the back panel with the open weave made in matching rouleau. The large ribbon roses in matching or contrasting ribbon embellish the deep V neckline.

Evening dress

This stunningly simple evening gown makes a dramatic impact using black grosgrain onto a red or white silk taffeta gown. Simply add bands of 38mm (1½") grosgrain ribbon around the bodice and skirt and top stitch them in place. The large cabbage, or folded roses decorating the bodice and skirt are made in a matching satin ribbon to the grosgrain ribbon.

Ribbon trimmed jacket

The elegant tailored jacket uses petersham ribbon to define the sleek lines of the lapels, pocket flaps and sleeves. This particular jacket design would look equally good using a contrast or matching ribbon.

Ivory and gold waistcoat

The gold lapels of this ivory silk
waiscoat are woven in 7mm (¼")
wide gold lamé ribbon in plain weave.
The 18cm (7") square panel on the
centre back is placed at an angle and
trimmed with a fine gold braid, hand
stitched in place. For added interest,
the braid was shaped into loops at the
waistline of the back and front. The
edges of the lapels are piped with
self-covered cording to give a professional finish to the neckline.

Bustier

The embellishment on this
bodice is quick and simple to
do, and great evening wear for
a young woman. The decorative
panel is of fabric and ribbon weaving,
woven on the bias with the raw edges
bound by a strip of rouleau. The panel
is then placed onto the centre of the
bodice and machined in place. A
profusion of gold lamé roses adorn the
waist and bust line.

Velvet waistcoat

This straight cut velvet waistcoat has been
adorned with a matching Russia braid and satin
rouleau. The leaf shapes are cut from wide satin
ribbon and bonded in place before being machined with a close satin stitch. Folded roses
using the 35mm (1") wide satin ribbon further
embellish the front and back. Use the same
technique as described for the evening jacket to
make the rouleau trimming.

Patchwork waistcoat

The detail on the back of this waistcoat is made from panels of plain weaving to form a patch-work design. This would look very striking in a simple black and white scheme – for the evening add large rhinestone buttons. Alternatively, try using strong jewel colours. Whichever you choose, use one ribbon to match your background fabric and every other colour you mix with it will become an integral part of your waistcoat.

Organza dinner shirt

Silk organza is such a wonderful fabric to work with and to wear – but you need a certain amount of bravado to wear such transparent fabrics for blouses! The design illustrated here is a super alternative to draw attention to a good figure and get you noticed. This design will look equally exciting in a lovely silk satin or Swiss cotton.

The ribbons used on the deep front yoke are the colourful 12mm (½") wide Swiss jacquard, and to achieve this pintucked effect on the front yoke simply lay the ribbon side by side 10mm (⅜") apart, giving an overlap of 2mm (⅛") on each ribbon.

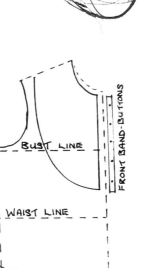

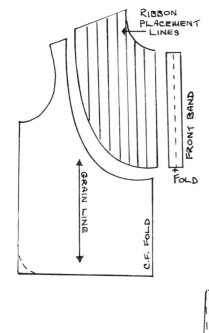

Bibliography

Further reading for those interested in the history of the ribbon weaving industry

Needlecraft Vols 22 and 63 (first and second series). Manchester School of Embroidery, 1900.

Master and Artisan in Victorian England. Evelyn, Adams and Mackay Ltd. 1969

Ciba Review 24, *The Basle Ribbon Industry*. Basle 1939.

Coventry in Crisis 1858–1863 by Peter Searby. University of Warwick Open Studies: Coventry Historical Associaiton 1977.

The Industrial Revolution in Coventry by John Priest. Oxford University Press 1960.

Author profile

Kay Anderson is an acclaimed author, fashion designer and international lecturer who has worked in the fashion industry as a designer and pattern cutter. As fashion and education consultant to a major world-wide haberdashery company, she designed educational leaflets and set design projects and competitions for young fashion designers. She also spent a year at Coventry Technical College lecturing full time on the many aspects of the fashion industry.

Kay's designs are often featured in popular magazines such as *Country Living*, *Vogue Butterick*, *Classic Stitches*, *Sewing World*, *Sew Today* and *Popular Crafts*. Her company, *Woven Treasure*, specialises in exquisite christening robes incorporating a range of beautiful embroidery designs which are sold throughout the world. Her work has been bought by royalty and the stars, including a special commission for Tina Turner.

Much of her time is spent giving talks and demonstrations at exhibitions around the country as well as in-store demonstrations for the *John Lewis Partnership*.

A fascinating video entitled *The Magic of Ribbon* (shown on *Sky TV*) is also available. With careful attention to detail, beautiful settings, lovely music and colourful textures created by the weaving techniques, this video is very watchable and is structured to make learning easy. For details of the video please contact Nexus Special Interests on 01322 660070.